MAND
THE MYSTICAL DIAG

MANDALA
THE MYSTICAL DIAGRAM OF HINDUISM

J.R. SANTIAGO

BOOK FAITH INDIA
Delhi

Mandala: The Mystical Diagram of Hinduism
J. R. Santiago

Published by:
BOOK FAITH INDIA

PILGRIMS BOOK HOUSE (New Delhi)
1626, Raj Guru Road Pahar Ganj, Chuna Mandi
New Delhi 110055
Tel: 91-11-23584015, 23584019
E-mail: pilgrim@del2.vsnl.net.in
E-mail: pilgrimsinde@gmail.com

Copyright © 2007, Pilgrims Publishing
All Rights Reserved

1st Edition
© 1999 Book Faith India

Artwork by Dr. Sasya
Layout by Naresh Subba

ISBN: 81-7303-183-5

The contents of this book may not be reproduced, stored or copied in any form—printed, electronic, photocopied, or otherwise—except for excerpts used in review, without the written permission of the publisher.

Printed in India at Pilgrim Press Pvt. Ltd. Lalpur Varanasi

Invocation

O Mother Goddess

"To those who adore thee, O Mother, thou grantest all boons.
Thou art the origin of the Vedas and of all the worlds. Be pleased to shine in my heart and accept my adoration. Thou art effulgence. Thou art the light of the Devas and Thou art in everything and beyond everything. Bathe me in Thy light and purify me"

— Mantra of Ayaty Varada Devi
from The Sandhya Upasana

Contents

Foreword		ix
Introduction		xi
1.	Hinduism	1
2.	Tantrism	9
3.	The Mandala	19
4.	The Yantra	35
5.	The Mantra	45
6.	The Tantra	57
7.	Sri Chakra	65
8.	Kama-Kala	83
9.	Analysis	93
Bibliography		98

Foreword

On a journey we come upon innumerable objects. They hold our attention briefly: there is only a casual curiosity, a perfunctory glance, and we move on.

It is only when something unattractive, unfamiliar, but enigmatic and interesting that we decelerate, take a closer look and try to understand it. Often there is no frame of reference to relate to it. There is only that intrinsic enigmatic quality that claims our interest.

A mandala is a work of art that belongs to this category of things encountered in the subcontinent of India. It is a strange artwork, but no doubt significant with symbols all over it and with a deity in the center. The real mandala is nondescript: it is just a simple diagram with geometrical patterns, which appears more like the drawing of a child.

In an art gallery or bookstore it must have some meaning, otherwise it would not be there.

Check it up.

It is called a mandala.

It is an object of ritual worship.

Worship?

As an object of art a mandala is comprehensible as an artifact of worship, but a diagram? There is only perplexity, for it is unusual for a diagram to be worshipped.

In the development of religious culture in India, as in any other culture in the world, new tools or techniques, invented or discovered, have evolved to serve as metaphors for metaphysical concepts — symbols with hidden spiritual significance. How they developed is lost in the mist of time.

A mandala is a symbol made up of a complex of other symbols, metaphysical in concepts, therefore abstract, incomprehensible and intriguing.

You are really on the threshold of an amazing discovery.

If curiosity takes the better part of you, you will find it, if not incredible or enigmatic, at least something new. It is very simple on the surface, but unintelligible. When comprehension dawns, however, it will speak volumes.

It will unexpectedly open up a vista of a vast panorama of the entire phenomenal universe. And involved in it are philosophy and science, even precision technology, and also psychology, and nearly all the related subjects in human existence and experience.

The mandala is not just an ordinary artifact of ritual worship, but certainly an extraordinary one, for worship requires extraordinary knowledge and control of the mind. It presents one of the profoundest aspects of Hinduism that is less known. It offers a new view of an entirely different human experience.

As in any form of worship it is the mind that links up with the Absolute, but on a mandala, for the worshipper's consciousness to tread the spiritual path to the ultimate, requires knowledge and precision. It is an aspect of Tantrism, and fundamentally connotes *maithuna* (coitus) which terminates in bliss — yoga.

It is mystical. The whole concept from its origin to its evolution is shrouded in mysticism that it raises more questions than answers on how this kind of knowledge has been acquired, but it is not within the scope of this brief exegesis on the mandala to discourse on the question.

This introductory work is simply to present a broad overview on what it purports to be: its concept of worship and what this form of worship entails in its totality. It is astonishingly vast in its ramifications.

Efforts have been made to present a simplified text on the whole complex form of worship to make it intelligible. Attempt has also been made to trace its origin and development. It has an elevated and sophisticated concept of worship for there is no appeal or pleading for material favor or physical security. It is a highly advanced form of worship.

The mandala's main component is the triangle. It is a basic figure in geometry, and hence, seems so modern, but really very old.

Even Neolithic!

Introduction

India — the subcontinent — has always been regarded as a 'bewildering enigma', a land of wonder and mystery that has deepened as it seemed to unfold. It continued to present an alien façade. It is indeed unique, unlike any other land in the whole world.

Life is lived close to nature, and it appears unorganized and therefore chaotic; but in its chaos there seems to be an undercurrent of order. It is the religious culture — the spiritual heritage — which makes up the underpinning of the whole superstructure of the Indian civilization. It has a highly philosophical culture, yet with the worship of nature still to some degree primitive. The ancient tribal creed has never relinquished its hold on its past, which reflects its continuous existence through the ages, from its evolution to the present.

It is this religious heritage which has made India a mysterious land, incomprehensible and unintelligible. The problem lies in the historical development of the creed of India, which has its origin in tribal folk cults, which were non-Aryan, non-Vedic, even non-Hindu, and therefore fundamentally indigenous.

It is this autochthonous tradition which continues to be the dominant influence in India's religious and social life. And to understand India is through her religious and spiritual heritage. This is the main key to the comprehension of its experiential and conceptual premises.

Its only intelligible cultural aspect is the Sanskrit link with the European language. This link provided the interest, which led to the investigation and analysis of the civilization and cultural aspects of Hinduism.

Interest in Indology deepened as translations of India's epics — of its vast literature — were made. Her myths and philosophies have been analyzed, along with the historical influences and traditional impacts on the evolution of her culture and civilization. In particular there was curiosity which inspired an in-depth study and analysis of India's creedal beliefs and rituals that proved amazingly to contain the essence of truth which inspired those on spiritual quest.

The scholars efforts have opened up an entirely new system of thought and experience, which for a long time remained rather incomprehensible to the rest of the world. They were successful in their endeavor and they have rendered attractive what was once objectionable, and engrossing what formerly was unacceptable. And this brought about an appreciation of another way of contemplating truth.

At first they naturally focussed on the Vedic heritage, but further investigations brought their academic research beyond the Aryan Age to the tribal folk cults — the origin of the spiritual life of India. Anthropologists succeeded in discovering authentic conceptual roots of Hinduism beyond the Vedic Age. Thus Hinduism has emerged a synthesis of the indigenous and the Vedic traditions. It is syncretistic in its evolution and development.

The folk cults have had heterodox tradition: new creeds or cult beliefs were superimposed upon the old ones, and with its eclecticism it became syncretistic. Their religious experience made them develop an inner inalienable reality: it made them perceive the Divine not as an abstraction but as a living experience.

This tribal perception of the Divine never faded away. The Divine remained the primary refuge, the essential dispenser of consolation, of hope and guidance: the arcane force animating and imbuing every stone and tree, every particle in nature with meaning. And to this day they continue to experience the Divine in terms of their primordial heritage.

The realities of daily existence and worship continue largely defined by non-Aryan, non-Vedic heritage, and therefore shrouded with the essence of the primitive, the arcane and the mysterious.

Now Hinduism presents incredible expanses of the mind hitherto uncharted by the rest of the world. And on the whole it is largely made up of creedal concepts and perceptions that is vast, varied and diverse. It is 'a nightmare vastness' unfolding in even more alarming varieties. This reflects a constant continuing interaction between man and his universe — the mysterious power beyond himself, the evolving or evolved vision of the Divine.

Religion is a basic human need and human spiritual experience is very precious. It is not merely to know the universe or the Divine but to understand and know himself that man developed his form of worship. This is fundamental in India's creed. Life bares human nature and reveals the stark reality of the human condition. The purpose was to unravel the mystery of human existence.

For this reason they take spiritual life quite seriously.

In worship or meditation they must have experienced the Ineffable in another dimension. The transition from pleading or beseeching the Almighty for material favor to the personal effort for liberation from the misery of this life must have taken a long time. It is an elevated aspiration, self-denying, and even renouncing the world just to attain salvation from the perplexing misery in life.

The Indologists have succeeded indeed in opening India to the world through her spiritual heritage, but really not all the way yet, but only so far, for truly there is still a great deal to discover to fully understand India. The principal spiritual concepts of India are already known, but even in this introductory exegesis it is surprising what new concepts could still be discovered.

And the mandala is one of them.

Let us hope it is the last — the last frontier.

Even then it is one of those 'nightmare vastness' that is mind-blowing and therefore mind-expanding.

The reference material on which this introductory work on the mandala is based has been generally taken from original manuscripts, and thus also mostly researched. They do not consist of the original experience or discovery of authors, whose works therefore differ on several aspects of the study of the mandala.

Even the original authors who wrote on the subject in Sanskrit more or less appear to have divergent views.

In its original form there must have been only one discipline or philosophy, but in its evolution new thoughts or philosophies must have sprung up, and further disciplines on the subject developed. It is not the purpose of this short work to go over the different schools of thought, but to introduce the mandala as an object of ritual worship. It is mainly to present a broad overview of the subject with sufficient details to make its significance clear.

The most important and indispensable is the basic motif of the mandala worship, presented for a comprehensive view of its fundamental concepts.

HINDUISM

1

Hinduism

Origin & Evolution

Man has lived on the bounty of nature as a root-crop gatherer and later as a scavenger. He progressed into meat-eating, became a herder of live-stocks, and eventually turned to farming.

The awakening of consciousness was gradual; he moved from one stage of life, as he became aware of the advantage he discovered, to a higher level of existence. For a long time he must have lived in the bosom of nature undisturbed. He was not stagnating; as survival stimulated his brain he evolved, but very slowly. Among the species he was the most intelligent and ambitious.

It was when he settled down and turned to farming that he began to encounter problems with unpredictable nature.

Sometimes rain did not come when expected; there was drought; and at times storms brought strong winds and heavy rains, which ruined his grainfields. Nature was wonderful, adorable, but occasionally awe-inspiring. Her benevolence could suddenly cease and bring in disaster. This was the beginning of his interaction with his universe. It was also the beginning of the awakening of his intelligence.

It began perhaps as an intuitive speculation that nature could be appeased or even appealed to for favors. With its wonders of perennial growth and regeneration, its perpetual transformation, man must have had a glimpse of the power or spirit of nature. The spirit of nature was feminine in character, and this was the beginning of the worship of the Divine Feminine

In the tribal primitive agrarian community the Goddess of Fertility evolved. They worshipped her in the form of a triangle, which is regarded as an element of Neolithic art. They offered sacrifices to appease her anger, but how they had conceived the Goddess as triangular in form is not known. It is a sacred form, which never faded away and has survived into the modern times.

In his fear and love of the Divine man's soul was being bared, but it also inspired his evolution. His talent in art was developing along with his intelligence. He drew animals before he knew the concept of art; he made primitive stone tools before he ever had an idea of engineering; and now his concept of the Divine was evolving before he ever had an idea of religion. He performed yajnas — sacrifices — and his invocations to Devi led to the evolution of his metaphysical philosophy: the sacred duty was adherence to the highest values in life.

Art is considered the 'truest mirror' of religion, and the spiritual experience as an emotional actuality produced a proliferation of deities, which acquired anthropomorphic features, but with supernatural powers. Images of these deities began to be drawn or carved in wood or stone, which were later endowed with bestial qualities, and theriotheism emerged for a while, but finally disappeared, replaced by deities with symbols of power. But these were only manifestations of the Divine Feminine.

The construction of shrines followed: they were primitive, small at first, which eventually became enormous and towering temples to house the deities. The name of the temple is *Deva Mandir*, which means 'God's Abode', but the folk cults called their shrines *Purana Mandir*, which means 'Old Temple', but in the tribal context it means 'The Dwelling of the Ancient Lore', which indicated perhaps that it was a repository of the accumulated religious knowledge they acquired through the ages, which means again that the shrine originally must have been a place where they did not merely offer sacrifice or worship, but discussed the forces of nature which perplexed them and which they tried to understand, which finally inspired the evolution of their Goddess.

In offering sacrifices to placate the spirit of nature rituals were developed, and the ones that were efficacious and which responded positively to their prayers were retained and perfected, until their rituals in worship began to be shrouded in mysticism.

Before the Vedic Age the tribal folk worship of nature was called *Sanatan*. In their worship and in their observations of nature and of life they realized that they had their own place in the eternal round of life. They may have had an intuitive glimpse of their own power, and they began to focus on their body, their mind, their life and their relationship with their world. This was the beginning of Tantrism.

The religious experience must have been satisfactory, but the form of worship, the offering of sacrifices to placate or to beseech for favors, material or spiritual, eventually changed. The social structure must have changed, and now it was no longer just the forces of nature they had to contend with, but the whole human environment. This must have been preceded by a degree of prosperity: the attainment of economic freedom must have redirected their spiritual effort to the liberation of the soul. The concept was abstract; it was no longer for physical existence, but freedom from *karma* and *samsara*, the cycle of birth and death.

The shift must have been a gradual but steady development. Worship became more sophisticated, the required knowledge now was vast. The struggle was now for the salvation of the individual soul. Community liturgy was not discarded, but the personal individual effort now took precedence.

Tantric worship of the Divine Feminine continued, but it was no longer the Goddess of Fecundity, but the Mother Goddess — the Absolute Force — in the universe that was worshipped. The crude Neolithic triangle, the embodiment of the Divine Feminine was retained. Over the millennia the worship of the Mother Goddess remained unaltered and unchallenged. The reason perhaps was that the spiritual experience of attaining self-realization or union with her must have been confirmed and authenticated by personal individual experience in the new way of worship that developed.

The new way of worship involved the mandala, the yantra, mantra and tantra, all of which fall under the term *vidya*, which means 'wisdom'. Worship in its origin and evolution produced this wisdom. The accumulated Tantric wisdom, considered the best and highest, distilled over the ages, is called Sri Vidya. It connotes not only knowledge of the Three Mysteries, i.e., the yantra, mantra and tantra, but also the underlying conceptual framework of the macrocosmic and microcosmic worlds.

And from here on the folk cult religious study of life and nature — the entire phenomenal universe — was to become very vast in its total ramifications. Their philosophy, science, principles, forms of worship, and their abstract concepts of evolution were already firmly structured and established before the Aryans came. The Tantric folk cults are very old, so old in fact that the cultic worship and practices had spread throughout the subcontinent, including the Himalayas and Tibet, and went farther towards China, Japan, and southeast Asia, and to the west to Egypt, Crete — the entire Mediterranean.

There were two known waves of pastoral Aryan tribes that arrived from the north to the subcontinent. The first waves were known as 'Wanderers' whose arrival date is unknown, but who appeared to have settled and developed into an agrarian community on the banks of the Saraswati River. This could be called the Old Aryan Age. And when the river dried up in 4000 BC they left in search for a better land, in the course of which they appear to have spread the Indo-European language.

The second batch of tribal pastoral Aryan that arrived in 1700 BC was known as 'Nobles'. They were regarded as primitive herders, but who spoke the language the natives understood, which indicate that Aryans had indeed come previously, lived there but departed. This old Aryan must have developed the original Vedic lore, which was transmitted through the generations by oral tradition.

It was during the period of the Second Wave of Aryans that the Vedas were for the first time put into writing. There is clear evidence that the indigenous spiritual culture had been taken up and incorporated in the Vedas: some of the Sri Vidya Tantric practices and worship are found in the Artha and the Rig Veda.

During this period the folk cult elements and Vedic beliefs were fused. Two creeds emerged: Tantric and Vedic. Initially they were in rivalry and in conflict, but in due course were fused together. The synthesis of the two traditions produced a syncretistic religious ideology identified as Hinduism.

The fusion, however, was fundamentally weak for the Vedic contribution was only in interpretation and symbolism of Tantra. It sought to transform Tantra to present an altered perception of Tantric traditions, but which in any event reasserted itself and become dominant. It retained its own symbols and significance and rejected what was alien to its native constitution.

The conflict between the two was more like a rivalry between theosophy and theology. The latter relied more on scriptures and interpretations, and the former was more practical: it had direct experience with Reality. It is mainly for this reason the Vedics could not hope to compete with Tantra's promise of *participation mystique.*

One and a half millennia later after the introduction of the Vedic creed, Tantrism still governed the mind and heart, worship and rituals of India.

Hinduism as it has developed is complex in its entire structure, metaphysical yet pragmatic, philosophical yet realistic but also mystical, with a ritualistic system in worship. There were inherent contradictions that were mutually exclusive yet frequently discovered inextricably welded, and beyond the rational have been somehow resolved.

It affirms life as an opportunity for improvement — for evolution and development — and has a cyclical view of time and creation. Its Tantric heritage is evident in the fact that it exalts the feminine and even sexual gratification, emphasizes the cosmic and is anthropocentric rather than theocentric. And it is tolerant of other creeds and accepts equally valid facets of truth.

The principles involved in Hinduism, particularly that of Tantrism, transcends geography and time, as they are applicable in daily life without infringing on other creedal beliefs. And life is perceived with no end, only a transition into different dimensions, cyclical in nature. It is not adversarial.

Its strength lies in its lack of dogmatism; it is resilient and tolerant of other beliefs, and has accommodated them within its own superstructure. It has evolved and developed through a continual progression of such accommodation, generally acceding to indigenous natural tendencies. It is syncretistic, but affirms the predominance of the indigenous tradition.

The preservation of this indigenous traditional heritage has made it possible for the great spiritual outlook of India to survive into the modern world and enrich the religious outlook in our time.

TANTRISM

2

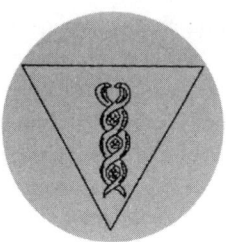

TANTRISM

During the Cold War period there was suddenly interest in the spiritual culture of India. It was perhaps because of the uncertainty or insecurity felt or the spiritual sterility developing in life. And there was a proliferation of yoga schools, meditation centers, and ashrams particularly in the west.

Tantra, as an aspect of the spiritual practices of India, apparently because of what was viewed as unsavory or hazardous practices, even in meditation, failed to become popular. Quite a few were turned off in taking up Tantra in their spiritual development. And only recently has there been renewed enthusiasm not only academically in the subject, but also because of its timelessness and universal appeal.

Tantrism is very old. Of its evolution and development, no written records, except for the Vedas, have been dug up. There are only archaeological ruins and vestiges of prehistoric or proto-historic folk art like those found in rural India and in Harappa, circa 3000 BC which attest to their indigenous origin.

There were evidently two waves of Aryan tribes that came at an interval of a couple of millennia. The first Aryans that came settled on the banks of the Saraswati River. Interbreeding perhaps made them absorb and assimilate native spiritual culture, but they left when the Saraswati River dried up in the middle of 4000 BC and searched for other land. And some of them must have settled on the banks of the Indus River where the Indus Valley Civilization, circa 3000 BC, also known as the Harappan Civilization emerged.

Here, Balaji or the concept of Shiva was already known. It is possible that during this time the spiritual culture was kept through the ages by oral tradition. In 1700 BC the second waves of Aryans arrived; they represent the New Aryan or Vedic Age, for it was during their arrival that the Vedas were written. It was only inevitable that the indigenous creed, along with their deities and practices, such as Tantra, was incorporated in the Vedas. There was a fusion of the two creeds. It was the attempt of the Vedics to superimpose their own precepts on the native creed that Tantra reasserted itself.

The Tantric worship of the Mother Goddess, which was widespread, with deep roots in the land, remained unaffected. It remained strong in the countryside, and the religious experience of the people with their mystical creed remained unassailable and fundamental. They remained cognizant of the sacred and their experience with it in their life.

Tantrism propounds a mystical philosophy, a way of knowledge, on which a way of life is based. It is one of the oldest methods of attaining a heightened consciousness and an expanded awareness, but its ultimate goal is self-realization or enlightenment. Its method involves scientific experimental process through which man can realize his spiritual potentials. It has an unconventional but spontaneous approach to life with its psycho-experimental system.

In Tantra the female principle is all-important. This is premised on the transcendence of Feminine Power. She is the focus of Tantric worship. Her nature is the leitmotif of Tantric speculations and metaphysics. Shakti represents the Feminine Power. It is a term, which means power, feminine power, dynamic creative energy. It is therefore also pre-Vedic and of indigenous evolution.

Shakti is also known as the Serpent Power or Kundalini, the cardinal vehicle of man's communion with the Divine.

The worship of the Divine Feminine began with nature's evocative qualities and character, which were maternal. Tantrism may have focussed on the female body, and her regenerative capability, and the worship of the *yoni*, her reproductive organ, began. Shakti, represented by a woman, was equated with Kundalini, the Serpent Power. In the worship of Shakti there was a sudden surge into the occult arts and mystical rituals.

How this developed is a question that is difficult to answer.

Tantra as it has evolved is highly sophisticated; it has an elaborate system of atomic theory, space-time relationship, astronomical observations, cosmology, palmistry, astrology, chemistry, alchemy, and discovered 'zero' which may have been taken from the concept of the *bindu* in evolution. Originally symbolized by a dot it has evolved into a cipher. It has also discovered psychic centers, the cosmic-cross points in the human body, and developed yogic disciplines supported by visual and abstract symbols.

It is not difficult to conceive of scientific disciplines coming under the scientific system of observation and investigation, but the discovery of unseen and undetected cosmic-cross points in the human body is mysterious.

It is claimed, however, that Tantra was revealed directly by Shiva himself, the Supreme Yogi, 'the Dark God of a dark people'.

Tantra is very old and it must have been the precursor of scientific knowledge in India. Attainment of scientific or even mystical knowledge was apparently based on intuitive insight, yogic visions, but also by observation and investigations for their preliminary or elementary postulates.*

> Note: *Science bases its investigation on observation and experiments susceptible or capable of verification.
>
> Diametrically opposed is another system called Tantra, which follows its pursuit of knowledge along *a priori* lines. Like science, the intuitive experimental method postulates certain facts; but unlike science it relies on spontaneous supernormal experience, which is tested in individual cases. It is a process of inference, not subject to any precise rules.

According to Woodruffe, "Tantra is from its very nature encyclopedic science. It is practical, and has no concern with worldly affairs. It lights the torch and shows the way, step by step, until the sojourner comes to the end of his journey."

It is scientific, experimental in its approach, not concerned with abstract representations but with practical ways to its objective. It is mystical, but the experience is verifiable by experiment. In a sense it is neither religion nor mysticism, but an empirical experiential method.

Shiva has no Aryan or Vedic association; his roots and antecedents are exclusively indigenous. He has been for ages, prior to the Aryans, the great god of tribal India, the masculine manifestation of the Divine Mother. He was referred to as 'Balaji', only an epithet, a euphemism applied to a divinity they could not understand, but the Aryans called him 'Shiva', the 'Gracious One', the 'Destroyer' as well as the 'Regenerator', the Ascetic no less than the Lover.

In a Mohenjodaro steatite seal Shiva is represented in an ithyphallic figure seated in a posture of yogic absorption. This reinforces the argument for his indigenous origin, also of the cult of yoga or Tantra. Shiva's *linga*, symbol of the phallus, represents eroticism, and thus it is also of folk cult origin along with the *trishula*, the trident (which represents the threefold power of the Divine), the Tantric rituals, yoga and the Goddess of the Fertility cult.

Tantra is a primitive phenomenon, very old and mysterious, with concepts of the Divine which have remained unaltered through the millennia into the modern times. It presents a new outlook. Its purpose is to bring an inner awareness of one's own self, and an understanding of one's relationship with the universe.

In Sanskrit 'Tan' means 'to expand' and 'tra' means 'to protect' or 'to guide'. It has, however, acquired different meanings. It is regarded as 'body', but perhaps in its esoteric significance is equated with 'thread', or 'breath', 'the sustainer of life'. It also means continuum, essence, or continuity.

Tantra is distinguished by no special sanctity, but only by a superior experience in matters of the occult. There was no intermediary, for the Divine was conceived as within man, a significant factor for the folk cult prodigious success. Tantra's essential impetus derives from the mystical character of its teachings.

Tantrism as a system began as a tribal form of worship when the essence of nature was discovered in woman. Thus began the worship of the Goddess of Fertility represented by a triangle. Tantra recognizes the female as endowed with all aspects of life, as the prime mover (dynamic energy) and generative in her procreative power. For this reason the female principle is called Shakti, who is identified with the Mother Goddess. In yoga she is also identified as the Serpent Power known as *Kundalini*. She represents the microcosmic version in the human body.

The Feminine Principle determines Tantric cosmology and ontology. It is the ultimate godhead. It teaches that each woman contains the substance of the Divine, and it also affirms man's innate divine nature, which when realized leads to enlightenment. The 'Divine Within' is the Tantric doctrine. The main Tantric spiritual discipline is the Kundalini Yoga, which requires a 'magic control of the Serpent Power'. It is called the 'Coiled One'.

Tantra defines the ultimate goal of the spiritual quest and charts the path to its attainment. In esoteric terms it is in reference to coitus or *maithuna*.

It is expressly sexual, but the sexual experience is sublimated. It is celebrating the eternal drama of regeneration. In worship the aspirant is like a lover going to join his beloved. This – *maithuna* – constitutes the solemn crowning, the all-redeeming moment of the Tantra sacrament.

The goal or objective is the consummation of the Divine Connubium, a return to the original and elementary state of oneness. This is the reintegration of the self with the Divine. This is the instrument of an erotic self-realization that belongs to the dimension of the sacred. This liturgic connubium is the ultimate spiritual experience. The divine union is yoga. For this reason *Kundalini* is called *mahabhoga* or 'great enjoyment' or yoga. *Mahasukha* means 'great delight'.

In *maithuna* is the pursuit of the sacred. It is the key to the ultimate religious experience. In Tantra therefore erotic enchantment and divine worship are defined as equivalent and concomitant.

In worship the purpose is to arouse the *Kundalini* or Serpent Power coiled at the perineum of the human body by the use of the mandala, mantra, or asanas or yogic exercises. When finally aroused the Kundalini or Shakti progressively reminds the worshipper of his own divinity and prompts him to make the ultimate union. A successful communion gives rise to self-realization.

In the process the macrocosm and the microcosm, the self and the world, the subjective and the objective are reintegrated. Differentiation dissolves, the ego is reintegrated with the Divine. This is the ultimate physical and mystical event experienced.

Tantrism accepts everything and denies nothing. It is to use all the energy available to realize the self. Tantra's discipline provides an experiential technique. Thus the individual must work alone on his self. His aim is to realize the intuitively known, the knowable within, the inner reality.

It places the responsibility in the individual like in any other creed, but it teaches that self-realization is possible – which can be confirmed – makes the aspirant steadfast in his resolve to attain not only enlightenment but final liberation. Once self-realization has been attained, the self-realized individual must live on a different plane: he must now preserve and maintain the spiritual and physical purity he has attained.

Central to its teachings is the concept that Reality is an indivisible whole: that there is unity in everything as a whole. The whole system – the macrocosm and the microcosm – is integrated as a whole. There is a dichotomy between the subjective and the objective aspects of the system, but they have a symbiotic relationship in which rests their unity, which can be observed only in worship.

This is based on the fundamental dualism in nature represented by the male and female principles: the male (*purusha*) is cosmic consciousness and the female (*prakriti*) the cosmic force of nature: the former is static and the latter is dynamic. With distinct qualities they appear different and separate, but they are in fact inseparable two aspects of a single principle.

Tantra therefore holds the belief that human beings (microcosm) and the universe (macrocosm) are one: that all that exists in the cosmos is also in the human body; that there is interrelationship based on their underlying unity in which external and internal energies are not polarized: they are not actually separate but are integrated into a cohesive whole. Thus the whole universe is seen as being in man and man being in the universe.

In worship the polarity is to be removed to realize the essential inseparability of the two, and the union that occurs is called Shiva-Shakti Yoga, a synthesis of the two in a state of equilibrium. In evolution the union of opposites produces the infinite diversity in the objective world. And this is mainly because of the existence of complementary forces, which attract or repel. For every conjunction of opposites bliss is produced. In worship this union dissolves consciousness in a blissful state. This in effect is self-realization.

Fundamental in Tantra is the psychological perception of 'consciousness as being' and 'consciousness as the power to become'. Worship is a psychic process: it is the force or power employed in the attainment of enlightenment; it is also the receptacle of enlightenment. It is this power that becomes aware of its attainment.

According to Tantra the world is deliberately established for the objectification of consciousness (*prameya*), while the individual is deliberately established as a mechanism for the subjectification of consciousness (*pramata*). Occasionally in conflict stress is experienced, but the reality of both is that they are inseparable. As in Kama-kala 'experience' cannot exist without 'existence'.

Tantra as a way of knowledge has also an integrated structure that covers both the macrocosm and the microcosm. How this knowledge was acquired, whether it started first with macrocosm or microcosm is not known. It could have begun either way. It must have begun at the microcosmic level —

the human body — the subjective and ended at the objective or macrocosmic level.

In connection with its central teaching or doctrine of the 'Divine Within' it must have discovered this principle in the human body, along with the Kundalini or Shakti, the Serpent Power* and the essential psychic centers called '*chakras*'** located in the spinal column. This knowledge is essential in Kundalini Yoga.

> Note* The serpent was also in the Garden of Eden. It enticed Adam and Eve to eat of the apple of knowledge.

> Note** The lotus, equated with *chakra*, is another indigenous symbol.
> "When the divine life substance is about to put forth the universe, the cosmic water grew a thousand-petalled lotus of pure gold radiant as the sun. This is the door or gate, the opening or mouth, of the womb of the universe. It is the first product of the creative principle, gold in token of its incorruptible nature."

The fundamental aim is to arouse Shakti to join Shiva. And to awaken the *Kundalini* is either by yoga (psychic), yantra (physical) and mantra (mental). There are other means, such as by *asanas*, or Hatha exercises, by *pranayama*, which involves the control of *prana*, the vital cosmic life force through rhythmic breathing process, and by Jnana (knowledge) yoga or by Bhakta (devotional) yoga.

Kundalini, known as 'The Coiled', is the dormant psychic power, regarded as the supreme force in the human body, a latent reservoir of psychic power. It is the central pivot of human psychophysical structure. When it is coiled it is asleep and man is aware only of his earthly circumstances. When awakened man is placed on a higher level of consciousness on the spiritual plane. In the language of modern science the awakening of the *Kundalini* means the activation of vast dormant areas called 'silent areas' of the brain.

Once awakened it rises up absorbing all the kinetic energy in the *chakras* and finally reaches the sahasrara *chakra* just above the head. When it arrives there a mystical event takes place: the Shiva-Shakti Yoga is attained. There is equilibration of the two in this synthesis.

Another way that is regarded as truly Tantric is the sexo-yogic technique: apparently 'one must rise by that which one falls'.

Sexual impulse become useful in opening the realities of the cosmos and in the realization of the oneness of the infinite and the finite, and the experience of joy or bliss with a woman. In concentration the mind is freed from contact with the outside world. The process includes the retention of sexual energy, which increases the inner pressure into a powerful energy that arouses the Kundalini.

This sexo-yogic practice becomes yoga, the means for spiritual edification. Sex is the physical basis of creation and evolution: it is the cosmic union of opposites: the male and female principles. In this form of worship woman is regarded as Shakti, in flesh and blood a goddess: thus she becomes the object of worship.

The First Principle of creation is the unfolding of love.

It is the fundamental basis of life.

Hence, the worship of love.

This is Tantrism.

THE MANDALA

3

THE MANDALA

In Tantrism the mandala is considered the basic matrix of the Three Mysteries or *Triguya* in ritual worship and in the attainment of enlightenment. The *Triguya* is made up of the yantra, mantra and tantra.

The yantra represents the spirit; the other two, the mantra is for speech or the soul, and tantra is mainly concerned with the psychic centers, the chakras, in the human body. They all have their origin and evolution in the Tantric folk cult known as Sri Vidya, described as having the best and the highest wisdom distilled over the ages. In the mandala worship all three are essentially employed together as a whole: they are not independent in this respect, but are interdependent upon each other. They make up together the essential elements in the ritual worship of the mandala.

This folk Tantric cult is pre-Aryan, but to be more precise pre-Vedic. It is therefore of considerable antiquity. It was indigenous in origin. It sprang up in the countryside from the original worship of the Goddess of Fertility, whose symbolic form was a triangle with lines etched across it. The original form of worship was the offering of a sacrifice. And over the ages it evolved into a mystical cult. Apparently Tantric practice was hazardous to the uninitiated and it has therefore been kept secret.

The worship of the Mother Goddess is central to the Tantric folk cult. Its main ritual worship artifact is the mandala, a mystical diagram, simple in composition and design, yet intricate and complex in its preparation and mode of worship. It involves abstract concepts of forces, power and energy of the macrocosmic and microcosmic worlds, of the evolution, preservation and dissolution of the phenomenal universe, and also of the mind and consciousness.

Involved therefore are not only art or symbols but philosophy, science, psychology and technology in the spiritual pursuit of enlightenment. In worship is the interaction of consciousness with the mandala to touch the Supreme, to be in union with the Mother Goddess, even if only for a fleeting moment, to feel whole, reassured, to realize the true Self.

The mandala is a circle, a symbol that represents eternity, wholeness, perfection, timelessness and protection. It is a universal symbol known in almost every culture and has the same significance. Prof. C.G. Jung theorized that this belief issued out of the 'collective consciousness' of humanity.

It is known particularly among tribal people like the American Indians in Mexico and California, and by the aborigines of Australia. Its aspects are shared by mystics all over the world. And now in the modern world it is employed in psychiatric hospitals to assist patients attain wholeness in their fragmented world.

The use of the diagrammatic mandala is also known all over the world . The followers of the Hermitic and Qabalistic beliefs made use of the diagrammatic mandala for the ultimate experience – the supreme enlightenment. Its mystical lore, the concept of the unity of the universe and of God, is also shared by mystics all over the world. This is though not common in Christendom for the Church has continued to be dogmatic, not pragmatic, when it comes to mystical or direct experience of the Divine.

In the subcontinent of India the worship of the mandala has thrived, flourished and survived over the ages. To survive for so long and remain the illuminating light to overshadow the Vedic creed the spiritual experience of the Divine must be real. And this established the continuum which links up the past with the present. It is then a living presence.

The divine experience is personal. It is individual. In worship the 'golden flower' — the divine spark — bursts forth in all its brilliance and splendor. It is the form of the Mother Goddess. The worshipper has attained self-realization, and he becomes aware that his human frame has become a temple of the Goddess.

This is one of the most amazing aspects of Hinduism. It deals with the philosophical and the scientific question of the evolution of the cosmos and of life that there are more profound questions than answers that crop up. The supreme question is how the ancient sages came upon this knowledge. They must have painstakingly struggled to know everything in their worship of the Divine, and analyze the nature, principles and function of the Absolute and the cosmos and of being.

All this must have at first been intuited, and when intuitive experience was sustained and confirmed by further experiments it became a fact. It is for this reason that the guru or worshipper must be competent, thoroughly familiar with the mandala, for worship requires precision technique, precise movement of consciousness in the mandala.

The diagrammatic mandala thus provides a spiritual passage into the supernatural — the mystical realm. It is an integrated system, and this is encapsulated in the fundamental principle of all existence and experience called Kama-kala: to exist is to experience; to experience is to exist. Beyond this there is nothing else. Both existence and experience are inseparable: they are eternal in their manifest and unmanifest forms.

In this individualized or personal form of mandala worship the motivating factor is revulsion which springs out of the experiences in life: there is desire not to return to *samsara* or under karmic influence. Central though in this spiritual effort is the attainment of self-realization, to know the nature of being, the real essence of existence, for reassurance which leads to enlightenment. It is the most unique form of worship in the world. The mandala, with the yantra, mantra and tantra, is one the most effective methods of achieving self-realization.

The mandala worship though involves a vast area of knowledge, the entire ramifications of which cover the entire phenomenal universe, its elements and of life. Philosophy, science, psychology and art and even technology must be known accurately. Precision in each aspect is required. And for which reason apprenticeship must indeed take a very long time.

The tribal primitive preoccupation with the forces of nature for survival and to the abstract effort for reintegration with the Absolute in the worship of the mandala appears so sudden to the modern mindset. The interval between these two forms of worship must have been very long. There appears always a quantum leap in the acquisition of knowledge which raises more questions than answers because it confronts the modern mind on how it all evolved and developed, for the knowledge is non-ordinary, extraordinary, uncommon, unusual, and the whole ramifications of knowledge and worship become indeed intriguing.

The basic theme of the mandala worship, in its ordinary and special form, in its yantra and mantra aspects, is the fundamental principle of all existence and experience known as Kama-kala. The central deity is the Mother Goddess who is called Tripura-Sundari or Lalita (the Ravisher), or Sri Chakra-Raja-Rajeswari, the very personification of this principle. The *Tripura* represents the body of the Mother Goddess.

It is a whole concept of existence and experience; it is not merely concerned with the primary process of creation, but involved also is the cyclical process of the universe's reappearance and disappearance.

The mandala represents the potent core of psychic energy, a balancing power the beginning of which is its end and its end the beginning. Within its perimeter is a complex of square, triangle, geometrical patterns which represent the Absolute and the paradoxical elements of totality. It is a 'paradigm of evolution and involution.'

In its formal structure a mandala consists of a few basic forms which remain fundamental. A circle with concentric circles usually with lotus petals enclosed in a square with four gates. It focuses on the totality of the cosmos, reflecting the cosmogenic process, the cycle of elements, and harmoniously integrates the opposites: the male and female polarity; the earthly and the eternal., It is a device for centering awareness and in fact represents the self of the worshipper.

The mandala is a mystical diagram. The term has two aspects: 'Manda' which means 'that which contains' and 'la' that 'which holds or defends what is contained.' It is also a process as it is known as 'mandam lati' that 'which gathers the essential details'. Technically it is a process involving power in a diagrammatic design.

It is used as an object of worship in liturgies and as an aid in meditation for the purpose of attaining real spiritual insights, or of acquiring material favors prayed for, and of activating latent supernatural forces in the human body. In the performance of rituals very strict rules were followed with precision. They must have discovered that when rituals were carried out in all their details accurately it produced a mysterious effect, which fulfilled their prayers.

Praises or hymns to deities were indeed chanted and it could be inferred that the gods granted them the favors they prayed for, but it was apparently in fact the accurate performance of a complete set of rituals that was considered the cause of the fulfillment of their prayers. The slightest inaccuracy in the performance of the rituals was not allowed. And because the folk Tantric ritual worship has been very effective and successful it has survived the passage of time.

Tantric Art

Tantric art, deeply concerned with the realities of life, is firmly rooted in spiritual values. It is visual metaphysics; its significance lies in the meaning it conveys; its foundation is worship.

The preparation of a mandala therefore is an artistic endeavor, but at the same time it is an act of worship. In this form of worship concepts and forms are created in which the deepest intuitions are crystallized and expressed as spiritual art. The design, which is usually meditated upon, is a continuum of spatial experiences, the essence of which precedes its existence, which means the concept precedes the form.

Spiritual values and beauty, the symbol of the divine, are woven into a significant idea: for 'form without content is meaningless; and content without form' has no definition. Tantric art is a projection of the outer and inner worlds of the artists. The act of creation is a contemplative process in which the seer and the seen become one.

In the mandala art the mysteries of the universe and the laws, which govern them are presented. Thus science and ritual together show the way to self-enlightenment. In Tantrism the way to the objective is 'within'.

Philip Rawson observes that the 'diagrams are meant to open door in the mind that reflects them, and so open for it a new and higher level of consciousness.'

Mandala art has other purposes or uses besides being a meditation device or an object of ritual worship. During festivals or ceremonies mandalas are made on the ground, on the floor and walls of houses, and in miniature forms are etched on palms as auspicious and protective signs.

The Mandala Preparation

The preparation of a mandala is a sacred act and involves elaborate and precise rituals. Precision is a requirement. Not anyone therefore can attempt or is allowed to make it. Only the competent, those with thorough and familiar knowledge, proficient in the methods of its preparation, are allowed to make a mandala. There are necessary qualifications needed, and requirements to follow: he must have impeccable credentials as an ascetic; he must undertake bathing and fasting to purify his mind and body; he must remain in seclusion for a period of time to be completely purified spiritually and physically; and he must meditate on his purpose and the design of the mandala.

The place of the mandala must be carefully chosen: the ideal site is near a river bank or the seashore, which must be to the north of the town, or it could be the proper chapel of a temple, which should be secluded. The day and time for preparing the mandala for liturgy must also be chosen. Elaborate rituals are made on the chosen site for the mandala to purify the ground, transform it into a power-place.

The diagrammatic design follows; it is the most important element of a mystical mandala. Even when solid artifacts, iconic, aniconic, symbolic, such as the divine weapons of deities are involved, it is the design of the diagram that is essential, important and indispensable. If the icon or solid artifact is immovable it is imperative that the diagrammatic design must be drawn before it; and if the icon is movable it is placed right in the midst of the diagram. The icon in the design then is ritualistically invested with power and the site of the mandala becomes consecrated ground.

In the process mantras are articulated or chanted to make the mandala charged with power. The chanting continues, as Sanskrit syllables representing deities are inscribed in appropriate places in the mandala. The Mother Goddess is central to the mandala-worship, but specific or particular deity could be consecrated in the design, or its portrait included in the diagram, if the mandala is for a specific purpose.

Mandalas made on the ground are usually destroyed when ritual worship is over. When the icons involved are immovable the mandala on the ground becomes permanent: continual worship invests it with power and need not be reconsecrated. New ones made on the same site has to be reconsecrated.

There are also mandalas that are solid, made of metal and three-dimensional, with a stupa or temple architecture, rising up to different levels, tapering off at the peak where the dot — the *bindu* — is located. These types are usually special mandalas of the Sri Chakra version, which is also known as Sri Yantra, regarded as the living supreme yantra.

Some mandalas are not meditated upon; others are made during the entire process of meditation. The first is mainly for the initiates as a model of familiarization; while the other is for worship. The most common mandala is generally made on paper or cardboard, usually kept and repeatedly worshipped or used as aid in meditation.

The Diagrammatic Design

It starts usually with a point, a dot, considered free from all dimensions. Apparently the dot turns into a line, but the usual practice is to draw a line near the dot. Other lines follow until they intersect, and geometrical triangular patterns are produced, which become symbols representing the male principle and the female principle.

Usually a primary triangle emerges ; three more triangles are made followed by five more inverted triangles, also intersecting one another which produce geometrical triangular patterns. This is the most common abstract design, yet the most important. A circle is drawn around the diagrammatic design followed by a square that encloses the whole diagram. This is the most common or ordinary mandala design.

The whole mandala represents the Mother Goddess and her manifestation, the phenomenal universe. It symbolizes Shiva-Shakti always uniting into knots in creation.

The Tantrics

Tantra recognizes the diversity in people as unavoidable and ineradicable due to karma, and it describes four psychological categories. And on this basis it prescribes in detail a particular liturgy for each type: the Kriya, Carya, Yoga, and Annutara. The purpose is not only to reveal the truth for salvation, but also to confer upon each category some *siddhi* or power.

The Kriya Tantrics are those devoted to liturgy in worship; the Caryas, noblemen, are those who combine liturgy with spiritual meditation; the Yogies belong to the royal family or powerful men, who cannot manage to renounce their possessions in this world, and to them a mandala with images of deities is recommended as a meditation device; the Annuttaratantras are the sinful ones, who do not distinguish good from evil, and who lead impure lives.

The four categories of Tantrics represent different types of passions; there are therefore four basic mandalas, each with special mantras and rituals. There are, however, hundreds of other mandalas, particularly prepared for individuals or families, based on their particular requirements.

Tantra is cognizant of the fact, based on the origin of the phenomenal world that the essence of life is primarily and fundamentally made up of kama, desire or passion. And passion for purity involves revulsion.

Kama-kala

Kama-kala, the fundamental principle of existence and experience, is a basic and integral part of a mandala. It possesses the three phenomenal processes: emanation, preservation and withdrawal of the universe.

The three gunas, sattvic (stable), rajasic (energy), and tamasic (inert), are reabsorbed and remain in inert but stable condition until re-manifestation in a solitary dot – the *bindu* or *bija* (source). They are the fundamental elements of the phenomenal universe and represent in a series of threes manifold aspects of the Mother Goddess.

In the reabsorption of the phenomenal universe there is only one dot – bindu – into which the universe has been withdrawn. This bindu is the seat of the Mother Goddess and represents Shiva in his inert and passive state. The three gunas, in their inert condition, have the potential of three essences: desire, light and sound.

When the inert state of the three gunas is disturbed, mainly by desire, it falls apart into three dots, with the potential of turning into lines to join each other and form the Primary Triangle or the kama-kala.

Desire springs up of its own accord, without any extraneous agency or stimulus, and is attracted to the rajasic dot representing dynamic energy or Shakti. And as it throbs it bursts into light, which, inspired (*vimarsa*) moves with a hissing sibilant sound (consonants) towards the tamasic dot, representing Shiva and the vowels.

As the inert *bindu* is pierced it swells and produces the primary sound 'Aham', a combination of consonants and vowels. This is symbolized by the word OM in Sanskrit. It represents the 'I' notion — the Ego. This primary sound produced the initial emanation or projection, which eventually evolves into the phenomenal universe. The sound preserves and sustains creation, and for this reason mantra is very significant in the Tantric mandala worship. The phenomenal universe is mainly made up of light and sound, and when its energy or rhythm ceases the entire universe is withdrawn, returned to the *bija*, the source, the tamasic point.

. desire

. light   . sound

The kama-kala triangle represents phenomenal elements and processes which alter the states or qualities or essences of the elements like the three gunas, which fall apart as points representing desire, light and sound, which have the potential of turning into lines as emanation, projection and withdrawal, eventually evolving into the Primary or Fundamental Triangle — the Kama-kala.

Symbolism

The dot represents the bindu or bija, the source; it is the residence of the Mother Goddess. The nine triangles represent the union of the male and female principles: four triangles for the male principle or Shiva and five inverted triangles for Shakti or the female principle. This union or yoga represents their inseparability, which is the fundamental significance of the mandala in Tantra.

The circle, which surrounds the diagrammatic design, represents the dynamic consciousness of the worshipper on the whole although it has other significance, i.e., protecting what it contains, the interior diagrammatic design being the most important in the mandala. The lotus petals in another circle represent generative power and principles. The square surrounding the entire design represents the physical world enclosed in four directions.

This is the basic mandala in its simplest form and symbolism. It represents the twofold drama of disintegration and integration. These two processes are also known as 'withdrawal' and 'emanation'. Yet, the mandala is actually a device or mechanism for reintegration with the Divine, for union to restore to the worshipper the ideal principle of things in life.

It is a paradigm of involution and evolution.

Worship

Mandala worship involves the community occasionally during festivals, which is officiated by a competent priest. On the whole though worship of a mandala is individual and thus personal. Like the priest or guru the worshipper must also purify his mind and body, and also must meditate on his purpose. The worshipper, usually a disciple, must also be proficient, with a thorough knowledge, in the mandala worship.

If he is a disciple the mandala worship is also a special occasion. It is an initiation, a rite de passage, in his spiritual path. Worship being individual and personal he is completely on his own. He knows that his salvation is only within him; it is his sole responsibility. He alone must go it alone, travel in the mandala.

Worship involves the gathering and concentration in the diagrammatic design the important aspects of the worshipper's world and his own psychological dynamics, for these two forces to interact. It is therefore a focussing of energies for their effective interaction. Its function is to project, create, integrate and transform. It is the worshipper's consciousness that functions here: it moves from one area of the mandala to the center to attain union with the deity or remove the dichotomy between his energy and that of the outside world.

The dot, or bindu, which is free from all dimensions means 'seed', 'sperm', or 'drop', the salient starting point, the gathering center in which the outside or external energies are drawn, and in the act of drawing the worshipper's own energy, the internal force, unfold and are gathered. The two energies represent the outer and inner spaces. The purpose in worship is to remove their differences and unite them.

In this union is yoga.*

Note* The purpose of the devotee in worship or meditation is not merely to beseech deities for material, or physical, or spiritual favor, or of attaining self-realization, but also for *siddhis* or supernatural powers, such as the power of becoming infinitely small to see even the inner structure of an atom, to become immensely large to even see the whole universe, to control gravitation, of leaving or entering the body at will, to master the elements and to acquire supper-audio power so that one can hear even the grass grow. There are other minor *siddhis* that could be attained, but in the spiritual path these supernatural powers are regarded as obstacles to the ultimate goal of attaining liberation.

The Disciple

In the transmission of knowledge the guru-disciple relationship is not intellectual: it is a relationship the mystics define as resembling that of a cow and her calf — between mother and child. It is a relationship in which there is complete faith reposed in the guru, and to whom the disciple is fully expected to be completely obedient. There is trust and confidence in the relationship

In this respect to become a disciple apparently is very difficult: there are tests to be passed, and for this reason out of the many who come to the guru, almost always only one remains: the one who has shown perhaps spiritual aptitude and complete faith in the guru. Disciples are chosen. The chosen one then lives with his guru, almost like a servant, for he must serve his master during his apprenticeship.

The guru in his wisdom brings to light gradually what is hidden in the depths of the chosen disciple. Tantric doctrinal preparations and the study of scriptures are made by the disciple to eliminate ignorance and perplexities in human experience. He undergoes initiation to remove ignorance due to human limitations. The disciple in his initiation has to visualize the primal essence of the mandala in its external form and then internalize it by contemplating on its psychic forces. The disciple is prepared for the return-trip to the Absolute.

The disciple who is to be initiated into the mandala worship must like his guru equally be purified in body-word-spirit as man is a product of three planes, the physical, verbal and spiritual. All these three must be integrated into one before passage into the spiritual plane can be attained. The disciple has to go through an ordinary initiation by means of elaborate rituals. The guru then prepares the disciple for the performance of the mandala liturgy, and a special mandala is prepared for him. To receive a mandala is the culmination of a long and patient apprenticeship. It is a proof or recognition by the guru of the disciple's spiritual maturity.

The essential point is the alignment of the energy of the initiate with that of the deity: it is to stay attuned with the deity.

After the *rite de passage* the *sadhaka* or initiate begins to regard himself as identical with God. Thus on his head is the symbol of the mantra 'Om', on his neck the mantra 'Ah', and on his heart the mantra 'Hum'. He begins to live on another plane, beyond *samsara*, the region of maya or illusion.

This is only a temporary adaptation of the spiritual reality. It is only a momentary transformation and integration. The struggle must continue until finally he is established as proficient in the mandala lore and rituals. And in his turn, perhaps, he becomes a guru himself, for him also to pass on his knowledge in a precise manner to another chosen *sadhaka*.

It is in this manner that the Tantric lore, in the mandala worship, is passed on from generation to generation with precision.

Meditation

The mandala is not only a ritual worship object but also a device which assists the worshipper in mediation.*

The purpose of worship is to beseech or appeal to the Absolute or a particular deity for a favor, material or spiritual. In meditation the intention is to realize the presence of the Absolute: the knowable in the heart. This is self-realization, which leads to spiritual development.

When the knower and unknown but knowable become one there is enlightenment.

Note* Scientific explanation: Physiologists in their scientific experiment have discovered that concentration on one point or on an unchanging stimulus called *ganzted*, a patternless visual field, or a stabilized image makes one lose complete contact with the external world.

The appearance of Alpha Rhythm in the brain as recorded in the electroencephalogram (EEG)) discovered that meditation is a 'high alpha state'. Conclusion: Meditation is neither esoteric or mysticism but a practical technique. This is a practical technique for purposes of relaxation. But this scientific experiment does not explain why mystical events take place in deep meditative state.

Significance

In the definition of a mandala lies its significance as a process: its function is to gather the 'essential details' and protect it. The essential details gathered and the energy or forces of the macrocosmic (the external world) and of the individual worshipper (microcosmic).

When it is consecrated with a deity it becomes a power-mandala — a sacred yantra — which takes over as a device for ritual worship and meditation.

As a yantra it remains a mandala with its specific function. It is where the energies or forces are gathered and concentrated for their interplay and interaction.

The Yantra

4

The Yantra

The yantra is a diagrammatic equivalent of the Mother Goddess. It consists of linear and spatial 'geometrical permutations' of the Goddess in the mandala: it expresses the eternal dialectics between the static and the dynamic — the idea of polarity — the concept of thesis and antithesis.

It has symbolic values: it represents an energy pattern made stronger by the precision in which the diagram is made. It is based on a mathematical method: reality is organized in terms of relationship of mathematical dimensions: the dot or bindu is the mathematical point of zero-dimension. It is the ultimate point of power, the repository of all manifestations, the bases of all vibration, movement and form. It controls everything. It is the starting point, but also the point of integration — the meeting ground — of both the subjective and the objective, the macrocosm and the microcosm.

In composition, the dot, lines, circle, triangle, square, are harmonized for equilibrium. It has a centrality, the dot, around which the rest is constructed. Enclosed in vertical and horizontal extensions it conveys a mathematical order and regularity.

It is a power-diagram in which creation and the control of ideas are said to be possible. The principle behind this is that just as each form is a product of energy pattern rooted in sound, in each visible form lies its own implicit power-diagram. It also symbolizes forces and qualities of the cosmos in elemental forms, and is therefore regarded as potent, not only as a conscious diagram, but symbolically consciousness itself. And interacting with it is the psyche or spirit of the initiate.

The completed mandala consecrated with a deity and initially worshipped is transmuted into a yantra. The yantra specifically refers to the geometric pattern in the mandala: it is the most important aspect in the mandala, but it is only an aspect of the whole mandala.*

> Note* Some authors equate the mandala, as the matrix of the Triguya, with the yantra. Others regard the yantra as something different from the mandala, and specifically describe the yantra as linear, made up of geometrical pattern, within a circle — the mandala.
> To avoid confusion the transmutation of a mandala into a yantra is the accepted interpretation: the two are not separate: in composition they make up the whole along with the mantra and tantra, the object of the ritual worship.
> Even the Sri Yantra or Sri Chakra, the supreme existing yantra, is based on the mandala.

Basic Yantra Geometric Symbols:
1. Point — This is the beginning; a series of points make a line, which signifies development like time or sound vibration.
2. Circle — This signifies revolution of planets, symbolizes wholeness and totality.
3. Square — This represents nature — the earth with gates in the four directions, which has to be transcended.
4. Triangle — This signifies the three worlds or modes or elements in the universe.
5. Two triangles — Two triangles intersecting each other represent union. When separated it signifies dissolution. Time and space cease to exist.

On completion of the diagrammatic design it is consecrated with a deity and the mandala evolves into a yantra: it becomes sacred, a spiritual or ritual device or mechanism for a specific purpose: an object of worship or as an aid in meditation.

In the consecration of a mandala it is actually in fact the intention of the designer that endows it with significance and therefore power. Initial worship turns it into a power-mandala — a yantra.

The process entails rituals to be performed: the placing or positioning of the tutelary deity (*kula devata*) alongside their captains (*nayika*), aids (*yogini*) and guards (*mudra-devata*) according to Tantric prescriptions and purpose of the worship. If no portraits or images are employed the divinity, along with the retinue of captains, aids and guards, is represented by appropriate Sanskrit syllables, regarded as sounds — mantras —emanating from the universe, each of which develops into a 'seed' syllable (*bija kshuna*), power or energy when inscribed in the mandala.

The yantra is basically a mandala, which has become sacred. In Tantra it now represents one of the Tripura or Three Mysteries: the spirit.

The Sanskrit term 'yantra' has two aspects: 'Yan' means 'to regulate' and 'tra' means 'to protect'. Thus regulation means protection. It therefore regulates the worshipper's psychophysical dynamics to protect it from disintegration, decay and death. In worship, which is intricate and mystical, the psychophysical energy of the worshipper is ritualistically regulated and protected by aligning it properly with the deity's energy.

This definition appears too simplistic but its ramification is fairly vast: it means just that — regulation of energy of the worshipper is protection. And this leads to spiritual development and enlightenment. Heinrich Zimmer wrote that 'it is a machine to stimulate inner visualization, meditation and experience.' This simple definition is comprehensive: this will become clearer later.

The Worshipper

The mandala is an instrument of worship in which human anxieties are made to disappear. But it is usually a mechanism for reintegration with pure consciousness for self-realization.

If the worshipper prepared the mandala for himself, after the ritual he will keep it in a purified place, in a room where no one except himself is allowed. The purified room becomes sacred. If it was commissioned it is simply given, not exchange for money or bartered for gifts.

The ideal recipient of a mandala is a disciple who is going to be initiated. On receiving the mandala it is not yet to him sacred: he must proceed to worship it to turn it into a sacred yantra.

Tantra teaches that man alone can work for his salvation. And in worship it is for man to confirm the doctrine of the "Divine Within'. Once this is experienced, even if only for an instant, Guiseppe Tucci wrote that it 'redeems the truth in us.'

'Truth is a personal conquest which one attains through a mystery,' he wrote in *The Theory and Practice of the Mandala*.

'It is a long and wearisome ascent during which one by one, there must be cast aside the impediments, the obstacles, the veils which hide the truth so that, at last, the sought-for light may dawn.'

In the mandala worship physical and spiritual purity is essential; it is indispensable if the worshipper is to identify himself with the deity. If he is not properly cleansed in mind and body he is not really prepared for worship. He would not be able to penetrate the obstacles and the *yoginis* would not be able to assist him overcome the impediments. Only the pure can identify with the pure.

He requires knowledge and initiation.

He needs 'real' knowledge, that 'which leads to cognition of ourselves and rebuilds the lost equilibrium. 'When knowledge does not transform life, and is not realized in it, it is not real. Initiation is essential to reinforce knowledge. It expels ignorance, and it completes the way of knowledge by causing 'the certainty of knowledge to pass into a permanent possession of the most durable experience.'

The Worship

The dot or point is the center of the mandala as well as that of the worshipper's being. The external energy of the outside world (macrocosm) as well as the worshipper's (microcosm) inner energy are gathered and concentrated on the dot.

In Sanskrit this process is known as *smrti* or absorption, which means the return of all energies in the phenomenal universe to the source, the dot or bindu or bija. It conveys not dissolution, but withdrawal or absorption of the phenomenal universe, which disappears into the dot.

Another process follows: the dot or point of absorption has also the inherent power in its nature to re-manifest the phenomenal universe. It is therefore the 'seed' of being, where the forces of transformation, multiplication, integration and harmony begin to emanate and fill the existential details of the worshipper and the experiential details of his world. This process is called *Srishti*, which means projection, emanation and creation.

The function of a yantra is to activate and direct energies of the outside world and of the worshiper. For this reason it becomes a psychocosmic mechanism, which relates the individual's consciousness in which thoughts abounds (*chittakasa*), the inner space with the outer space in which things subsist (*mahakasa*) in the comprehensive and integrated space to remove the subject-object dichotomy (*chidakasa*).

In this manner the world is viewed as an element established deliberately as an object of consciousness, while the individual is viewed as a subject of consciousness. In the latter stress is experienced, but which is also for a purpose, and which is even regarded as something expedient. It is to eliminate this stress and integrate and harmonize the outside world (*mahakasa*) with his own consciousness (*chittakasa*) in the space of individualized consciousness.

This is the simplest form of yantra-worship; the purpose is to unite the individual (microcosmic) consciousness with the outside world (macrocosmic) energy; it is to remove the difference between the object and subject — the macrocosmic and the microcosmic. In the main it is the worshipper's consciousness that moves around the yantra until harmony and integration of the two forces is attained in the bindu, the dot in the center of the yantra.

This dot is the starting point, the meeting place of two forces, but it is also the terminal point when harmony or yoga is attained.

This is the main motif of worship or meditation. It is always to merge in union (yoga) with the super Ego, pure consciousness, the Absolute, for enlightenment or self-realization. When worship is successful the dichotomy is dissolved and union or yoga, a state of ineffable peace is experienced.

The purpose of worship, whether on an ordinary yantra or Sri Chakra, is the same, except that in the latter it becomes more technical and intricate; it requires more knowledge and proficiency in the processes of worship. In the Sri Yantra all symbols of the Triguya are projected and the process of worship becomes more involved, and consequently is regarded as a higher or special form of worship.

The purpose is also changed in the Sri Chakra yantra: it is now simply to dissolve the difference existing between the worshipper and the Mother Goddess or Shakti to be able to make a complete identification with her for self-realization. The goal is self-realization.

Ritual of the Bhuta-Siddhi

This is a ritual for the purification of the elements. It is a great aid to mental process of identification. In Tantrism this is a preliminary ritual to the actual worship. This involves the dissolution of the grosser elements of which the body is composed. It consists of reciting the following appropriate mantras:

For the Earth element	– *Om Hrim Prthivyal Hum Phat.*
" " Water element	– *Om Hrim Adbhyah Hum Phat.*
" " Fire element	– *Om Hrim Tepase Hum Phat.*
" " Air element	– *Om Hrim Vayave Hum Phat.*
" " Ether element	– *Om Hrim Akasaya Hum Phat.*

These mantras act on the mind of the worshipper until the material body is purified. It is a step-by-step process. Along with the gross elements the subtle (*tanmatras*) cosmic principles, and all the organs of the senses and intelligence stuff (*mahat*) are also dissolved into *prakriti*, and a gradual mental process of involution takes place. It is claimed that only after dissolving the body or being can the *sadhaka* acquire the capacity to begin the proper ritual worship.*

Note* In this case he is already in a meditative state, which means already in union. Consciousness is lost for the mind ceases to flow, but there is the observing self which remembers the condition attained. All that is required is the physical and spiritual purification.

Yantra As Psychocosmogram

The preceding psychocosmic yantra-worship is the simplest or most ordinary or common form of mandala worship. Yantra as a psychocosmogram is more complicated, but the presentation here is also broad but simple, more like the preliminary introduction to the Sri Chakra, also known as Sri Yantra, the supreme living yantra.

In this psychocosmogram yantra the universe (macrocosm) and the individual worshipper (microcosm) are presented. The entire phenomenal universe is symbolized by a graphic design alone or in combination with an icon. The worship of the individual turns the yantra into a device for transformation, projection, concentration and integration. Thus, the worshipper's consciousness finds expression in the yantra, which helps expand it beyond the subject-object dichotomy.

The diagrammatic design of a psychocosmogram yantra is more complex. Around the dot, the gathering point, is a pattern of geometrical triangles which crop up, each having a definite character and specific role as symbols.

The triangles represent the male principle; the inverted triangles the female principle; the circle enclosing them the individual's consciousness; the lotus petals around the circle the regenerative power and principles within the inner space, which stands for the worshipper's consciousness; the square for the physical world, bound in four directions.

The entire yantra, representing the phenomenal universe, is the playing field of the worshipper's consciousness, which moves in and out of a series of enclosures, through entry and exit ways in the circle at cardinal points. Yet, the entire yantra represents the Mother Goddess. It is sustained by her power and compassion; it is her emanation and sporting ground as well. In the play of the worshipper's consciousness it seeks to remove the obstacles or dichotomy between the macrocosm and the microcosm.

This cosmographical diagram is a potent symbol of simultaneous evolution and dissolution or involution, in tension yet in repose. In yoga the meaning is secret, but it is universally known to involve simultaneous perpetual motion and perpetual rest represented by the circle and the dot. The former is Shakti and the latter is Shiva. These are opposite forces only embodied in the Mother Goddess.

The yantra worship essentially requires an in-depth knowledge of the mind or consciousness, also familiarity with the Tantric scriptures regarding the Absolute, and of the origin, evolution and even elements of the phenomenal universe.

It is the worshipper's consciousness, his intention and purpose, mainly because of his familiarity, knowledge and therefore proficiency in the ritual aspects, which have to be accurately followed, that moves in his worship in the yantra as his playing field. He must therefore be conscious of his awareness of his own being and of his world.

He deals with symbols, abstract concepts, usually unseen yet knowable in the technology of the yantra. His method must be scientific, intellectual, also artistic and psychological. In the end he comes upon something, a mystical event, beyond the rational.

The Mantra

5

The Mantra

Mantra as a word-power sound delineated here pertains to the science as well as the philosophy of the Sanskrit language.

It is an articulated word; articulation is expressed by sound; thus mantra is a spoken word, but in this context with a special meaning. Here, mantras are regarded as divine names preceded by letter (*bijaksaras*) which are regarded as indeclinable seed-sounds. It is divine power clothed in sound.

Like in any other language the word must be pronounced with the proper tone, accent or rhythm, otherwise it becomes incomprehensible or vague and confusing. And everything that is involved in a mandala must be done with precision as a science or technology in worship.

Mantra as a discipline is one of the *Triguya* or Three Mysteries involved in the preparation and worship of a mandala. The term mantra has two aspects: 'Man' means 'the mind or speech'; and 'tra' means 'to guide or to protect.' Thus it means protection or guidance of the mind.

As an integral part of the *Triguya* it is the most subtle and encompassing it covers in detail the whole range of the phenomenal universe and of life. Its symbolism covers a very wide area and could be forbiddingly complex, which is beyond the scope this introductory book. Only the essentials along with the necessary details, to give a comprehensive overview of the subject will be covered.

Mantra is an indispensable discipline in Mandala worship. It means 'that which when reflected upon gives liberation.' It is a revelation of the Mother Goddess in sound. Sound is the soul of form which emerges into life through sound from inside out. Sound and form are interdependent; every form is a vibration; hence, every sound has visual form — a wave. Everything in the universe, animate and inanimate, is made up of vibration of a particular frequency. Mantras also have their color-forms, and when articulated properly its visual correlates begin to manifest.

Mantra must be repeated to create a wave pattern (*japa*), accompanied by an understanding of its meaning and a proper articulation of its syllables. Each syllable or letter is charged with energy, which causes vibrations in the inner consciousness. Sound vibrations are manifestations of Shakti and are thus equated with deities. Mantras are 'seeds' of power.

It has a dynamic power-pattern rooted in sound, and this is the essence of a yantra. For this reason, in the preparation of a mandala, mantras are chanted, and as syllables representing deities are inscribed in the yantra. It is therefore in essence a sound equivalent of a deity.

In silence is the potential of sound. Sound is conceived to be the specific quality of space. The basis of sound is the mechanical impact, which generates vibrations in molecules of the object struck, which hit surrounding molecules of air to produce it. And it expands as waves.

In Tantra there are three kinds of sound:

1. Sphota — This is the transcendental sound, inaudible described as the 'unstruck sound.'
2. Nada — The supersonic sound.
3. Dhvani — This is the audible sound.

It is believed that sound has to pass through several stages before it is heard: 1) *Para*, 2) *Pasyanti*, 3) *Madhyama*, and 4) *Vaikhari*. These are apparently equated with the phases of evolution.

Tantrism is cognizant of sound as energy, and its central doctrine on sound is called *Sphota Nada*. This is the foundation of Tantric mantras. The primary sound is known as '*Para-Sabda*'. Its vibration creates light and space-time. Sound varies in pitch, rhythm, volume, frequency, speed and harmony. If the right chord of the octave of an object is struck it can be animated, remodeled, or even destroyed. Thus the vibrations of rhythmic repetition of certain sounds (syllables) is believed to awaken psychic fields in the human body. The Tantric mantras are built on this principle.

Dr. Hans Jenny wrote of vibration: 'And always it is the underlying vibrational processes that sustain this unity in diversity. In every part the whole is present or at least suggested.' This is similar to the Tantric teaching that everything is everywhere, even in particles.

The mantra involved in Tantra is Sanskrit, an Indo-European language, a fusion of the Indian indigenous tongue and the Aryan language. *Sanskrita* means 'polished', complete'. As in other languages sound units constitute the Sanskrit alphabet. How they are classified or categorized differ from language to language. In Sanskrit the classification of sound units differ to some degree with other languages: in Sanskrit sound units have been classified in great detail and given symbols representing it appears the entire phenomenal universe.

There are, for instance, fifteen vowels in Sanskrit from short 'a' to the unmodified nasal 'm', which are regarded as representing the male principle or Shiva. From five of them, i.e., A, I, O, R and LR evolved five groups of consonants, i.e., the gutturals beginning with 'Ka', palatals beginning with 'Cha', cerebrals or unguals beginning with 'Ta', dentals beginning with 'Ta' and labials beginning with 'Pa'. The consonants represent the female principle or Shakti.

The five groups of consonants have each five syllables. The 'Ka' group represents the primary form of matter, i.e., earth, water, fire, air and akasa or ether; the 'Cha' group represents the subtle form of the same matter; the 'Ta' group stands for five organs of action, i.e., speech, apprehension, locomotion, excretion and reproduction; the other 'Ta' group denotes five sense organs: visual, auditory, olfactory, gustatory and tactual; the 'Pa' group represents the mind, ego, consciousness of the female principle of action, change and growth, and the consciousness of the male principle. These twenty-five consonants represent twenty-five principles of existence.

Other consonants evolved out of these five groups of consonants: Ya, Ra, La and Va represent principles of attachment, wisdom, projection and illusion. There are others, but altogether there are fifty letters in the Sanskrit alphabet: fifteen vowels and thirty-five consonants, and they are claimed to range the entire universe of existence and experience, of illusion and reality, and of the empirical and the transcendental order.

The consonants for expression are dependent on the vowels, which provide power, for consonants are in the nature of mere seeds. When fused with vowels consonants forming words acquire meaning; otherwise they are simply meaningless sounds. And for consonants to be transposed into *matrikas* — mother-like words — the vowel power along with the thirty-seventh sound principle is added. The word power 'Sri' is added to the letter.

Example: *Vidya* means wisdom, but when 'Sri' is added it becomes *Sri Vidya* — the best and highest wisdom.

The dimensions which bound the universe in its unmanifest origin (Shiva) and its manifestation (Shakti) are illustrated by the entire letters of the Sanskrit alphabet from 'a' to 'ha'. The universe, therefore, as experience is simply made up of sounds which constitute the alphabet. The fifteen vowels are counted as one principle; the thirty-five consonants as thirty-five principles.

Altogether there are thirty-six principles that underlie the constitution and function of the universe. Another is involved in an unmanifest manner: this is the underlying principle of the other thirty-six manifest principles, and altogether there are thirty-seven principles.

The articulated sound, designed to obtain, or to crystallize and communicate knowledge concerning the most fundamental principles governing the universe, is in Tantra designated as *vidya* — wisdom — an aspect of the Mother Goddess. Some mantras, regarded as the best vidyas, are very secret.

The entire Sanskrit alphabet is called *Devanagari, 'Divine Abode'. It is considered mathematically and psychologicaly perfect, and thus* represents the Mother Goddess: the vowels stand for her head and its details; the consonants for her limbs and vital currents in her body. Therefore *vidya* as sound of the alphabet means an aspect of the Mother Goddess. There are three vidyas: *maha-vidya, vidya,* and *siddha-vidya.* The first is meant only for advanced initiates, the second for the ordinary ones, and the third for those involved in magical skills, witchcraft and sorcery. This *siddha-vidya* is also known as Sri Vidya.

The fifty letters of the alphabet are also represented by the moon, sun and fire — by their light which sustains the universe. The moon stands for the vowels; the sun for twenty-four consonants; and the fire for ten consonants. These three also represent the Mother Goddess: the moon as her head, the sun as her torso, with the fire at her feet. She also represents three powers: the power of cognition, action and intention.

Tantra affirms that the creative force of the universe, the Mother Goddess, is present in all the letters of the Sanskrit alphabet: the different letters symbolize the different functions of that creative power.

In Tantrism words and their meanings are eternal. The connotation or significance of a WORD DOES NOT DEPEND ON HUMAN CONCEPTS BUT ON THE NATURE OF THE WORD ITSELF. The word is regarded as eternal and therefore its meaning is also eternal. Like the mantra OM.

'I' — ego — in Sanskrit is 'Aham'. 'A' stands for Shiva and 'ham' for Shakti. Aham is the unity of the two. And the two are in the ego sense of man. Mantra therefore is not merely a combination of sounds, but is the subtle form of the Goddess. Hence, the purpose of meditating on the mantra is to identify the self with the Goddess.

There are several versions of the mantra, all dependent and varying upon the purpose of the devotee: it is either for illumination, emanation, preservation, absorption or integration, or for the indeterminate state. Another is for meditation: to free the mind of normal thoughts but active in the spiritual practice. There are other versions of the mantra, which, because they are so powerful, require the practice of virtue, discipline and even rituals. Some mantras are forbidden to householders, but there are some particularly prescribed for them.

Some primal mantras, such as OM, are in fact so powerful they stimulate and awaken latent forces in the human body. The uninitiated is admonished to mentally utter them. Some therefore have become very secret. Authors of some Tantric text admonish the gurus:

"Do not impart to the undeserving this sixteen-lettered lore, even if you are threatened with death. This lore must be guarded as a great secret like one's private parts. When the devotee's mind gets absorbed in the feet of the guru, like salt in water, it is only then that the great *vidya* is to be communicated to him out of compassion."

This knowledge is said to be the hidden or secret significance of all the Vedas, Shastras, the Puranas and the Yamalas.

The seed syllable, the sound of the alphabet, are as symbols very significant and important. They represent a correlation of the various phases of evolution and its termination. Thus whoever is proficient in mantra is considered to have mysterious power.

Not anyone can use mantra. He must have proficiency in its employment, an understanding of their secret power; they must be spiritually atttuned.

The parts of the whole mandala are represented by syllables of the Sanskrit alphabet — from the dot or bindu to the lines, corners or triangles. To the devotee the three most important in the rituals are the seed-syllables 'Ka' from which everything arises and which confers the highest benefit of liberation; 'La' which brings him prosperity; and 'I' which secures his happiness: these are the very substance of the mandala worship.

According to Bhaskara-raja, an authority on mantra, there are manifested meaning attached to mantras: general sense, traditional meanings, secret teachings, pragmatic meanings, etymological meanings, explanations based on word power, etc.

There are those, he wrote, "who merely know how to articulate the mantra without understanding the meaning thereof are like donkeys carrying loads of sandal wood; the utterance of words without a knowledge of their import will not lead to any accomplishment, even as ghee — purified butter — poured on the ashes will not help light a fire."

There are two broad ways to understand the meaning of mantras:

1) Explanations of the essential symbolism and the verbal imagery involved;
2) Communication of practical significance meant to guide the devotee in the ritualistic details and in the rituals contemplative discipline.

Most of the ancient authorities rely on the primal or traditional meanings, which provided inspiration for the Vedas. It is for this reason the Tantra Sri Vidya mantra symbolism is believed to go back to 'hoary antiquity' — pre-Vedic.

The mantras are now represented by Sanskrit alphabet. The traditional expressed sounds had been taken up and transposed into letters of the Sanskrit alphabet; they have remained in their original sound, for the mantras have to be articulated loudly with the proper tone, accent or rhythm to establish resonance or rapport with the particular deity invoked.

They could not be changed; they are unalterable for their power and dynamism have been proved as effective, and hence, have survived the passage of time as invocations in ritual worship or in meditation.

Mantras as Sanskrit syllables of the alphabet are inscribed in the mandalas, each symbolizing the power of the Mother Goddess. The two decorative parts, the square (*bhupura*) and the triple girdle (*tri-vrtta*) are left out. In each of the lotus petals one of the sixteen vowels is inscribed: 'a' at the entrance, and the others moving in sequence in an anti-clockwise manner. On the eight lotus petals consonants from 'ka 'to 'ksha' are inscribed. These two groups of lotus petals signify the conjunction of Shiva and Shakti.

In each corner is inscribed a letter with composite seed-syllables. The same is done to the other corners, and also the corners of the primary triangle. The central point has no inscription; it is beyond both visual representation and verbal expression. When, however, the purpose of the worship involves the swelling of the point the foundational male-seed syllable OM and the seed-syllable IM of the Mother Goddess are inscribed.

The nine chakras in the yantra are believed to evolve from the inscriptions of the letters of the alphabet: from the letter 'I' which stands for the union of kama and kala, the bindu, the central point evolves. This is the first chakra. From the seed-syllable 'Hrim' the primary triangle and the eight-cornered figure arise; from the letter 'Ha' (occurring thrice) and the letter 'E' arise three chakras representing preservation aspect; and from the letter 'Sa' (occurring twice) emerge the two groups of lotus petals. The letter 'La' occurring thrice gives rise to the square (*bhupura*).

OM

In the beginning the origin of sound is the union of the male and female principles, and the fundamental principle of this union is known as kama-kala. The union produced the primal sound 'Aham' or Ah-hum' symbolized as Om in Sanskrit, a combination of vowels and consonants. It is the creative power in the phenomenal universe. It is the basis of cosmic evolution. All the elemental sound-forms of mantra spring up from this eternal sound. Its reverberation permeates and pervades the entire cosmos: its rhythm is the strength that sustains, nurtures and protects it.

It is the holiest and most powerful mantra; it precedes all other mantras; it must be articulated first before the start of any project or undertaking. It is the Mother Goddess manifesting symbols. It corresponds to the basic three elements created by the primary implosion (the Big Bang theory): the spirit-mind-body.

This supreme sound is the very essence of consciousness. It is therefore the mantra in the Ajna chakra — the Third Eye — the site of consciousness, which is cognizant of things as objects as well as of itself — it is self-aware. It is the essence which provides power to the worshipper's consciousness in his ritual worship. It is made up of a combination of light (consciousness) and energy (Shakti).

Combined with the mantra is *prana*, regarded as the cosmic energy; it represents the hidden life of God and of things, and therefore is in everything: it is considered the 'universal breath' with the quality of repercussions and differentiation which produces infinite number of things.

OM is inherent in life. It is regarded to exist before and after creation. It is imperishable and therefore is the symbol of the Infinite. It resides and is present in Silence and represents the entire manifest and unmanifest universe. Sound springs up from the depths of the void and returns into it. What is existential is therefore only experiential.

Worship

In the first phase of ritual worship images of divinities were etched in the mandala, but because they were considered merely ornaments, regarded as representation of the artist's concept or interpretation of the deities, it has only an instrumental value in its unmanifest essence. They were therefore replaced by syllables of the Sanskrit alphabet: the syllables contain the secret essence or 'seed' of the deities.

It is enough to concentrate on the syllables to evoke the divinity, but no evocation can occur unless the symbols have been contemplated upon or visualized for a long time. The inscription of syllables in the mandala is done with their articulation. The whole power is in fact done with the chanting of the syllables from the very beginning to its termination.

The start of the worship begins with the disappearance of the cosmos; the worshipper's consciousness contemplates on the reabsorption aspect and returns the phenomenal universe to its source — the dot known as *bija*. This is done according to a precise and subtle alphabetic scheme that is articulated as mantra.

The second phase of the ritual worship, more like meditation, is on the emanation aspect of the phenomenal universe. It is the conscious use of the syllables, articulated properly as mantra that brings up the various phases of the worship.

The Tantra

6

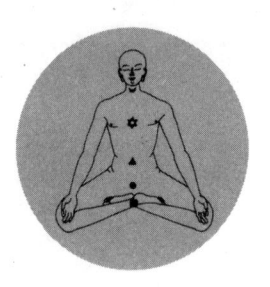

THE TANTRA

The Body Mandala

According to Tantric philosophy the creative power is not only in sound but also in the human body, that the microcosm is an exact replica of the macrocosm. Thus the divine power in sound and elements of the universe are also in the human body.

In fact the essence of the Mother Goddess is also in man. This is mainly because she has three phenomenal forms: the universe, the human body, and the alphabet of articulate speech (*varnamala*). The latter two are regarded as miniature universes. She is called Lalita, the Ravisher, or the Playful One: her lila or play is the creation and preservation of the universe.

The whole philosophy of Sri Vidya, the highest wisdom, is known as Tantra, but the particular study of the human body in respect to its abstract parts, the subtle energy centers called the chakras is described as Tantric, perhaps because the mystical lore started with the study of the human body and human consciousness.

In Tantra the phenomenal universe is regarded as an integrated structure sustained by the Mother Goddess. The Sri Chakra yantra, along with the mantra, is a concrete model of this integrated structure. The human body is also viewed as an integrated system, which possesses all the essential dimensions of the universe. The Tantrics believe that the entire universe unfolds itself in the development of the individual: as the human being evolves so does the universe apparently; but the individual as he evolves perceives more of the universe, which is seen as unfolding.

But the universe represents diffusion or expansion and therefore separation (*vyastati*), while the individual represents compactness (*samashti*) or focussing. The presence and power of the Mother Goddess could be clearly discerned at the individual, the microcosmic, than in the universe or macrocosmic level.

In Tantra the human body is analogous to Mt. Meru: it has a base which supports the spinal column, the *Meru-danda*, the column along which chakras are located. Mt. Meru, the resplendent abode of the Absolute, the highest peak in the center of the universe, which illuminates the four quarters with its lusters, is the model of the human body mandala. The body mandala represents the human physical constitution. The resulting geometrical patterns produced by intersecting nine triangles, four for Shiva and five for Shakti are made to correspond to parts of the human body, which is presided over by the Mother Goddess.

The body-mandala is represented as a fortress of the Mother Goddess. Hence it has ramparts, entrances, guards, lines of defence, areas of succour, corners, arches, garlands and courtyards. Thus ascent is very difficult: the purpose is to unite with the Absolute, in Tantric parlance in connubial bliss. Apparently it is a sexual act, but spiritualized.

Temples and stupas were also modeled upon the architectural shape or form of low mountains dear and sacred to the Mother Goddess. In Tantra the central point of Mt. Meru is also the central point in the human body — the spinal tube, the *sushumna* in Kundalini yoga, which leads to the Sahasrara chakra.

The body-mandala is a Tantric model. This is now a Sri Chakra yantra mainly concerned with the human physical constitution in its essential and abstract structure, most particularly with the spinal chord or column (*meru-danda*), the column of Mt. Meru where the Brahma *chakras* are located. There are six *chakras*, energy centers, and each is symbolized by a lotus, color, element, female deity, mantra, etc.

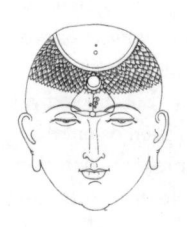

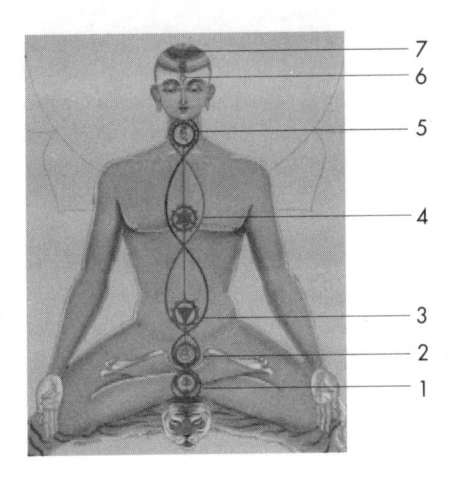

1. Muladhara Chakra. This is known as the foundation or root-support.
   It is located at the perineum, the seat of pleasurable experience, the source of physical desire. It represents the earth element, and is symbolized by four lotus petals.
2. Svadhishthana Chakra. It is known as the 'Goddess' Own Abode' (Shakti). It is located in the area of the sexual organ. It represents the water element and symbolized by six lotus petals.
3. Manipura Chakra. This is known as 'Jewel-Filled' and is located in the area of the navel. It represents the fire element and is symbolized by ten lotus petals.
4. Anahata Chakra. This is known as the 'Unstruck Sound' and is located in the heart; it represents the air element, and is symbolized by twelve lotus petals.
5. Visuddha Chakra. This is known as the 'Specially Purified' and is located behind the throat. It represents the akasa or ether element, and has sixteen lotus petals.
6. Ajna Chakra. This is the 'All-Knowing' or commanding chakra. It is located between the eyebrows. It represents consciousness, and has two lotus petals.

7. Sahasrara Chakra. This is the 'thousand-petalled lotus'. The site is controversial: some say that it is within the head; others claim it is four-finger breadth above the cavity of Brahma. The latter claim apparently is true, borne out of experience for this chakra has been called the 'Citadel Without Support' (*nivalamba-puri*) — the residence of the Mother Goddess.

The entire Sri Chakra of the body mandala symbolizes the physical form of the Mother Goddess.

Each of the chakra from the bottom up is presided by a deity: Brahma, Vishnu, Rudra, Isvara, Sadasiva, and Paramasiva.

The chakras in groups of two along with their divinities represent three aspects of the Mother Goddess:

1. Muladhara and Svadhishthana chakras represent emanation;
2. Manipura and Anahata chakras represent preservation;
3. Visuddha and Ajna chakras represent absorption.

In the Tantric body mandala the human body chakras are graphically represented: the square (*bhupura*) and the triple girdle (*tri-vrtta*) represent the muladhara chakra or emanation (*srishti*); the sixteen-petalled lotus (*ashta-dala*) outside the main diagram correspond to the Svadhishthana chakra, which represent preservation (*sthiti*). These two chakras surround the diagram and in fact preserve it.

The fourteen-cornered figure (*chatrudasara*) and the outer and inner ten-cornered figure (*bahir-* and *antar-dasara*) correspond to the manipura chakra and represents absorption (*samhrti*). The eight-cornered figure (*ashtara*) and the Primary Triangle (*trikona*) together correspond to the anahata chakra.

The central point, the bindu, in its visible form represents the Visuddha chakra, and in its invisible aspect the ajna chakra. The process also involves the proper placing of the tutelary deities alongside their captains (*nayika*), aids (*yogini*), and guards (*mudra-devata*). Images of retinue divinities are replaced by Sanskrit syllables that are inscribed as mantras.

The transcendental significance of this Sri Chakra yantra goes beyond the ajna chakra, for the seat of the Mother Goddess, the thousand-petalled lotus, is beyond the individual and the phenomenal universe. This is the peak of Mt. Meru above the cosmos.

Worship

In the worship of the body-mandala the muladhara and the svadhishtana chakras are omitted, apparently because they are regarded as dark worlds. Thus, from the manipura till the sahasrara worship is conducted from center to center: the worship on the manipura leads very close to the fortress of the Mother Goddess; at the anahata the worshipper gets into the fortress and beholds the Absolute at a distance; at the visuddha he is helped to approach the Mother Goddess in close proximity; at the ajna it will make him acquire the same form as the Mother Goddess. The most important goal is the sahasrara where he attains union with the Mother Goddess. This is the center of the highest bliss — the *parananda*.

Thus, the worshipper must meditate on the identification of this peripheral area with the central point.

The moon, sun and fire further correspond to the three involvement of conscious transactions: of cognition (*prasnana*), subject of cognition (*pranata*) and the object of cognition (*prameya*). And further the three instruments of knowledge: the individualized consciousness (*buddhi*), the ego (*ahamkara*) and mind (*manas*); and again the three values of life: dharma according to divine law; *artha* (wealth) and *kama* (pleasures).

The square (*bhupura*) represents the cot (seat) of the Mother Goddess: the four legs stand for the four principles underlying the phenomenal universe: emanation, preservation, dissolution and withdrawal into the subtle and hidden state. The plank or seat represents the fifth principle — the reception and retention of the phenomenal universe in the seed-state until re-emanation occurs. The four principles are incorporated in this fifth principle in the causal and latent potential form.

The process followed here is introspective visualization that invests the mandala with meaning or power. This involves the gathering of the individual psychological dynamics (*chittakasa*) and the reflection of the Absolute. There is a focussing on the Mother Goddess in worship or meditation.

When a yogi who has acquired spiritual power makes the body-mandala and consecrates it the mandala becomes a yantra, but for ordinary worshipper it is a powerhouse from which he can draw and enrich his inner world.

The body-mandala is designed like a fortress, which the worshipper must penetrate. In worship he must reach the highest point – the *sahasrara*. The function is to activate the latent forces within the external diagram and the worshipper's own psychological constitution.

The body-mandala becomes a yantra, which leads the worshipper to unite with the Mother Goddess. Meditation or worship on the yantra is designed to achieve identification with the fundamental forces of the cosmos or the Mother Goddess. The individual consciousness must identify with the cosmic consciousness and the initiate must journey alone in the mandala to attain union or oneness with the supreme Divine Mother. This leads from darkness to light – the brilliance and splendor of the thousand-petalled lotus.

Sri Chakra

7

Sri Chakra

The Sri Chakra yantra represents all the fundamental principles of Tantric philosophy. It is therefore known as Sri Yantra, the best or supreme existing yantra. It is also known as Nava Chakra for it consists of nine triangles.

It represents Shakti's own form, powers and symbolizes her manifestations. This is therefore exclusively the worship of Shakti. It is distinguished as the supreme yantra because it projects all the Triguya. And it can only be conceptually understood by careful and gradual analysis till one begins to comprehend it. It is described as 'the vast dense mass of consciousness ' leading to bliss.

It is regarded as a visual masterpiece of abstraction. And it is believed it was created through a 'revelation' rather than by human ingenuity.

Sri Chakra literally means 'The Wheel of the Mother Goddess'. The Sri Chakra mandala is a visual representation of the Mother Goddess: the mandala design symbolizes her court, which has entrances, enclosures, and pavilions, along with the places of all the aids, guards and attendant deities. It is essentially for the worship of the Mother Goddess.

The place of the Mother Goddess is in the center of the design; the bindu or dot is represented as her seat which has four legs representing deities responsible for the creation of all things: Brahma – the creator is in the northeast; Vishnu – the preserver – is in the southeast; Rudra, for withdrawal, is in the southwest; and Sadasiva for retention, in the northwest.

The dot or bindu represents the principle of emanation, projection, preservation, withdrawal and retention of the withdrawn universe until recreation. These five principles are five activities (*pancha kriya*) of the Mother Goddess: they are her five modes of expression, regarded as five inert dimensions or 'ghost-like' (*pancha preta*), which become alive or dynamic only at her inspiration.

She is the life-giver. The deities under her, including Shiva, her consort, are like corpses (*sava*). Bereft of her inspiration Shiva is unable to move, but inspired by her he becomes Kamesvara, the effective master of desire. It is only then that the phenomenal universe is projected, preserved, dissolved and withdrawn, but retained in its unmanifest state until manifested.

The Sri Chakra represents the male-female dualism but also their union. The worship of the Mother Goddess is fundamental, central to the Sri Chakra, and therefore the male principle is subordinated to her. Thus the male deities are passive and the Mother Goddess dynamic. Inherent though in their nature is the principle of inseparability (*avinabhava*). This is the fundamental significance of Sri Chakra. It is the central motif, the cornerstone of the Tantra philosophy.

The ultimate male principle (*purusha*) and the ultimate female principle (*prakriti*) are united in the central point — the *bindu*. This is Shiva-Shakti yoga. Shiva, the male principle, represents the principle of consciousness, while Shakti, the female principle, the principle of dynamic energy. In this union or relationship the male is passive, the female dynamic.

The yantra is now transmuted into the body of the Shiva-Shakti yoga; the male principle is represented by a triangle, the apex of which points away from the worshipper; the female principle is represented by an inverted triangle with the apex pointing towards the worshipper. These male and female aspects are now described as *chakras*.

Diagrammatic Design

The diagrammatic design of Sri Chakra is essentially a pattern of nine interwoven triangles, four of which represents the male principle (*Shiva*) and five inverted triangles representing Shakti, the female principle.

The nine triangles also represent nine basic elements or root substances (*mula-prakritis*) of the universe. In the human body they are regarded as nine substances: five from Shakti, i.e., skin (*trak*), blood (*asrk*), flesh (*mamsa*), fat (*medher*) and bone (*asthi*) The four from Shiva are: semen (*sukla*), marrow (*majja*), vital energy (*prana*), and the individual soul (*jivatman*).

The primary triangle has three angles, hence it is called Tripura, the Mother Goddess, who holds three fields. This is a projection of the central bindu representing the unmanifest yet immanent union of Shiva and Shakti.

The interwoven nine triangles illustrate further this union in a manifest manner, and produces forty-four other triangles: actually only forty-three but including the center of the bindu altogether forty-four. This pattern of forty-four triangles constitutes the main design of the yantra.

Surrounding this pattern are two concentric circles with lotus petals: the inner one has eight lotus petals and the outer has sixteen. These in turn are girdled (*valaya*) by three other concentric circles. These are enclosed by a square field, usually called the courtyard: this is the inclusive 'earth-stretch' (*bhupura*) in the form of three lines signifying an enclosure. On each side of the square is a gateway (*dvara*) in all four directions.

The angles (*kona*) produced by the intersecting triangles are very important: they signify points of union of Shiva and Shakti. They represent the many projections of the central point, which is enclosed within the fundamental or primary triangle — the kama-kala — the residence or seat of the Mother Goddess in her aspect as Desire.

In Sanskrit the angle, enclosed on two sides but open on the third, is that which makes articulated sound (*kunati, vadayaty amena*) possible. It is also regarded the 'top of a weapon' (*astrasya agram*), the weapon being the Sri Chakra design.

Meeting points of intersecting lines are also important, significant as being sacred. The point where two lines intersect (*sangam*) is called *sandhi*; where three lines meet the point is called *marma*. The *sandhi* has the form of a vagina (*bhaga*) and symbolizes *sandhana*, the act of union. It is an expedient (*yukti*) element. The *marma* is a vital spot that has to be guarded, for it is the seat of life (*jiva-sthana*), its very nature (*swarupa*) or essence (*tattva*).

The central motif of the Shiva-Shakti yoga is expressed in pairing off of various geometrical forms in the yantra: the dot or bindu with the primary triangle; the eight-cornered figure with the eight-petalled lotus; the ten-angled figure with the girdle of the sixteen-petalled lotus; and the fourteen-petalled lotus figure, the *chatur-dasara*, with the enclosing square. It is for this union that the entire design is called *yogini* (aid), the power that assists the worshipper to attain union with the Mother Goddess.

There are altogether twenty-five psychophysical principles fundamental to existence and experience; the union of Shiva-Shakti is the twenty-sixth principle, which is unmanifest but pervades the whole yantra design.

In Sri Chakra the nine chakras or enclosures represent emanation of the universe (*srishti*); its preservation (*sthiti*); and its withdrawal (*samhara*). Three chakras: 1) the square, the sixteen-petalled lotus, and the eight-petalled lotus on the periphery, together constitute the center of emanation; 2) the fourteen-cornered figure and the two ten-angled figures, the inner and outer, in the middle, the center of preservation; 3) the eight-angled figure, the primary triangle and the central point, make up the center of reabsorption.

The first three chakras are presided over by chandra, the moon (the head of the Mother Goddess); the second group of three chakras by Surya, the sun; and the third by Agni, the fire. These three groups of three chakras, known as three fields, compose the triad — the Mother Goddess as Tripura — are fundamentally inseparable.

This represents the basic theme, the significance, of the Sri Chakra yantra: the union of Shiva and Shakti represents three phenomenal processes: emanation, preservation and withdrawal of the phenomenal universe. In the inert state or condition the union is unmanifest but immanent.

The Making of a Sri Chakra

The Sri Chakra mandala is considered the best and supreme yantra, and for this reason the conditions and processes involved in its preparation are very restrictive, in particular as to who, where, when and how it should be made. On the whole the general requirements in the preparation of an ordinary mandala as regards the design or his disciple, the site chosen, the time to prepare it, and how to prepare it apply to the Sri Chakra mandala.

The requirements of a Sri Chakra though are raised a degree higher, for preparation and design and rituals are highly technical.

The mandala designer must be proficient in Tantric lore, and must know the two ways of counting the nine enclosures in the mandala: first counting starts from the central point outward towards the square; the second counting starts from the outside the square towards the central point. This knowledge is not merely required in its preparation, but also in conducting ritual worship on the yantra. He must therefore know the ritualistic details involved.

It is for this reason that the preparation of a disciple begins from an early age to understand and be able to visualize the wide-ranging symbology.

He is also expected to be a devotee, an ascetic, steadfast in his devotion, who must bathe and fast to become spiritually and physically purified as the preparation of the mandala is regarded as a sacred act. He must also for a certain length of time remain in seclusion and meditate on the design of the mandala. He must therefore be a *sampradayavit* — a truly competent guru. His first concern is to bring out the universality inherent in basic forms, and he releases what he has experienced inwardly in his meditation.

The preparation of the Sri Chakra mandala must be carefully done with precision, in particular with the interior design, specifically called the yantra, for any error in the main portion will preclude the descent or investment of power in the mandala. The interior design is very important for it is the central area — the *bindu, trikona* and *ashtara* — which is invested with power. Great care need not be taken in the design of the two lotuses, the three concentric circles and the outer square for they do not constitute the integral part of the yantra, although they have their own ritualistic symbolism and significance.

There are apparently quite a few methods followed in the preparation of the Sri Chakra mandala: there is no standard procedure, but there is generally a sequence followed in preparing it.

There are two main disciplines called the Kaula and the Samaya methods. The former follows by starting with the line of absorption; the latter the line of emanation. Further differences between the two methods are in regard to the posture of the primary triangle and the position of the central point or bindu.

In the Kaula method the primary triangle points downward and the bindu is in the midmost part. In the Samaya method the primary triangle points upward and the bindu is situated in the mid-most part of the six-angled figure. The Kaula discipline disregards the number of angles important to the Samaya discipline: it only holds important the points where three lines meet called *marmasthana* formed by nine triangles.

In both disciplines the eight-petalled lotus and the sixteen-petalled lotus, the three concentric circles, and the square are important. In other methods they are simply added as ornaments as they are not included in ritual worship. In still other methods these peripheral details are regarded as important as the nine triangles

In spite of these differences among these divergent methods of worship they all appear effective; and what appears essential is the precision applied in the system of worship particularly in the important focal point of the yantra — the geometrical configuration enclosed in the circle.

Besides the diagrammatic design there is also an iconic Sri Chakra known as Meru, because it has the form of a low mountain (*andha-meru*). It maybe in stone, crystal, gemstone, wax or metal, i.e., gold, silver or copper, but not lead, iron or zinc. In this meru form the chakras are projected on different elevations of the yantra. This appears to be the model of the stupa, which is also a mandala.

There is also a variety of this Meru Sri Chakras for different devotees:
1. Where the layout emphasizes emanation from the central bindu it is called *meru-prastana*, prescribed as suitable for hermits, celibates and the less-evolved devotees;
2. Where the layout is more on preservation, called *bhu-prastana*, it is suitable for pious householders;
3. Where emphasis is on dissolution, it is called *kailasa prastana*, and is prescribed for ascetics and renunciants.

Significance of Evolutionary Processes:

The dot or *bindu* falls into three parts caused by the throbbing of desire: these are the three *gunas* which fall apart whirling and forming the three basic vibrations.

The Primary Trinagle is formed by the three gunas: it stands for the three aspects of Shakti: Bala, the Young One; Tripura-Sundari, the Beautiful One; and Tripura-Bhairavi, the Terrifying One. It also represents the threefold process of creation: emanation, preservation and withdrawal.

In the expansion of space and time, sound and energy, the primary triangle is transformed into a series of lines, more triangles, circles and squares. They are in fact modifications of OM the primal vibration.

Significance of Nine Enclosures Worship

In Sri Chakra worship is done on the nine enclosures of the yantra. The worshipper has to visualize the whole mandala as a fortress, in the innermost part of which resides the Mother Goddess. It is his consciousness, which moves towards this sanctum sanctorum, through successive enclosures (*dvarana*) with the phenomenal and psychical projections, which illuminates the path he must follow.

Each of this enclosure is regarded as covered, a station or step in his onward journey; with each step he moves closer to his goal and increases his identification with the Mother Goddess. Each has its own name, a characteristic physical form with a specific spiritual significance, its own color, a presiding divinity, a class of *yoginis* (aids) in this spiritual movement towards integration and a divinity who welcomes and purifies the worshipper.

In this Sri Chakra worship the *yoginis* assume a special role or function: they make explicit the sequential union of the male and female aspects in each enclosure. As aids to the worshipper they mainly derive their power from the Absolute, whose presence in his heart confers this power on them. Tradition has it that these retinue divinities of the Mother Goddess number sixty-four crores or 640 million. In worship there are sixteen important *yoginis*, but only three are very important: Bala, Tripura-Sundari and Tripura-Bhairavi.

The Sri Chakra is the body of the Mother Goddess who pervades the phenomenal universe as adorable power and resides in the individual as pure consciousness. Worship of the nine enclosures actually reveal her true form consisting of a series of graded significance, universal and individual, ideological and ritualistic, expressive and experiential. These nine circuits, regarded as chakras, indicate successive phases of worship. The worship sequence begins with the square (*bhupura*) and is completed at the innermost enclosure in the central point.

First Enclosure

This is the square called the 'Deluder of the realms', with portals in four directions, in which esoteric knowledge is transmitted and diffused. There are actually six gateways with the addition of 'above' and 'below' entry points:

a. The Eastern Gate is the path of the mantras;
b. The Southern Gate is the path of devotion;
c. The Western gate is for rituals;
d. The Northern gate is the path of wisdom.

First Enclosure

The other two: the 'below' gate is the path of words; and the one 'above' is the path of liberation. The one below is identified with the southern gate and the one above with the northern gate.

These gates are taken to correspond with the chakras in the human body: 'below' corresponds to the muladhara chakra; the eastern to the svadhishthana, the southern to the manipura, the western to the anahata, the northern to the visuddha, and the 'above' to the ajna chakra. This symbolizes the initial part of emanation. This is the stage when desire springs up in the devotee.

Second Enclosure

This is the lotus of sixteen petals called the 'Fulfiller of all Hopes'. It represents three human values: virtue, wealth and pleasure. The petals correspond to sixteen vowels, one each starting from the east in an anti-clockwise manner. It corresponds also to the muladhara chakra, and this symbolizes the second part of emanation. This is the stage when he moves towards his objective.

Third Enclosure

This is the lotus with eight petals called 'Agitator of All'. The eight petals represent psychophysical dynamics. In the east it stands for speech and expression; in the south apprehension and reception; in the west locomotion; in the north body urges and elimination; in the southeast, pleasurable feelings; in the southwest rejections and reactions; in the northwest attention; and in the northeast detachment and dispassion. They correspond also to eight consonants beginning with 'Ka'. It also corresponds to the manipura chakra and symbolizes emanation-preservation. This is the stage when one succeeds in moving towards one's goal.

Third Enclosure

Fourth Enclosure

This is the fourteen-cornered figure called 'Provider of all Prosperity'. It represents the first fourteen letters of the Sanskrit alphabet. It corresponds to the anahata or heart region. It signifies the first part of preservation-emanation. This is the stage when hope rises in the devotee.

Fourth Enclosure

Fifth Enclosure

This is the ten-cornered figure called 'Achiever of all Objects'. It corresponds to the visuddha chakra at the throat. It signifies part of preservation denoting 'preservation-preservation.' This is the stage when possibility of inner realization is felt or discerned.

Fifth Enclosure

Sixth Enclosure

This is the ten-cornered figure called 'Protector of All'. It corresponds to the manipura chakra, but apparently situated between the eyebrows, the site of the ajna chakra. It is in the nature of fire and symbolizes the third part of preservation, denoting 'preservation-absorption'. At this stage the dawn of inner realization is perceived.

Sixth Enclosure

Seventh Enclosure

This is the eight-cornered figure called the 'Remover of all Diseases'. It is represented by the five letters of the 'Pa' group, and also the letters 'sa', 'sha', and 'sa'. It symbolizes the first part of absorption, denoting absorption-emanation. It corresponds to the forehead or the svadhishthana chakra. This is the stage when devotee is freed from earthly bonds and is at the threshold of the inner circle of realization.

Seventh Enclosure

Eight Enclosure

This is the Primary Triangle called Kama-kala, the immediate effect created by the central bindu. This is known as the 'Bestower of all Attainments'. It is described as the 'wandering between horns' — the two lines that meet below and the horizontal line that touch these two lines on top suggest movement between them. It represents the head of the Mother Goddess symbolizing three Tantric centers, three dots with the potential to form a triangle. It symbolizes three fundamental tendencies of existence: desire, knowledge and activity. This is the stage before self-realization is attained.

The center symbolizes the second part of absorption, denoting absorption-preservation. This Primary Triangle is white or pure sattva.

Eight Enclosure

Ninth Enclosure

This is the central point or bindu called 'Filled with all Bliss'. The Primary Triangle is merely the manifest form of the bindu. The point is the actual yantra in which the Mother Goddess resides. This is the sanctum sanctorum, abounding in joy. Worshipper participates in the mystical union.

The center is known as the 'Field of Deliberation', the indissoluble union of the subjective-objective counterparts of experience — the 'I' or ego and the 'This' — Shiva and Shakti.

This central point has three dots that are arranged in the form of a triangle. They represent three fires: of the moon, red in color, representing the *ida* channel on the left of the human body; the sun, white in color, representing the *pingala* channel on the right side of the human body; and Fire, of mixed colors, representing the central channel, the *sushumna*.

Ninth Enclosure

This symbolizes the gathering up of emanation: the central point becoming three is an act of swelling (*ucchuna*) which turns into the Primary Triangle in the Sri Chakra. It represents absorption-absorption, hence it is described as 'filled with all bliss'. Bliss is defined as 'resting in oneself'. This corresponds to the sahasrara chakra, the *brahmananda*, the aperture on the crown of the head.

Worship of Sri Chakra

The worship of Sri Chakra comes in three forms: Gross or physical which involves the worship of the yantra; the second deals with the subtle and abstract which involves meditation on the symbolism of the mantra; third is mental or transcendental which is regarded as purely Tantric.

In the worship of the yantra the Sri Chakra is represented as the image of the Divine Mother or Devi.

The worship of the yantra, internal and external, the practice of Kundalini yoga included, and other *sadhanas* or meditation, constitute the

Tantric way of worship. The chief Tantric mantra is *Pancha-dasaksari*, and the chief Tantra is meditation on the Sri Chakra. The entire yantra, mantra and tantra together is regarded as the embodiment of the Mother Goddess.

Worship is an orderly psychic movement to the inner core. In this process the Sri Chakra yantra is like a mirror which reflects the inner self. It is a spiritual pilgrimage. The object of worship is the transformation of acts of ordinary experience into forms revealing the play, power and bliss of the Divine Mother in such a way that whatever is naturally done is transformed into worship in daily life. This presupposes union with the Mother Goddess — this means self-realization has been attained.

The *upasaka* or worshipper must follow certain disciplines: he must not criticize the spiritual path of others, and must be steadfast in his own. He must do *japa* — the chanting of mantra beads — as an undercurrent at all times. He must not ask for favor or accept them. He must do his duties in the world and his worship of Devi without attachment to fruits. He must be fearless; must not acquire wealth or possession with selfish motives; and he must consider nothing higher that the realization of the Self.

The goal of all spiritual practice is the discovery of man's identity with Reality. The ultimate reality is Sat-Cit-Ananda — Existence-Consciousness-Bliss. The essence of man is identical with this Reality. It is because of the existence of the ego, the 'I' notion that the difference is experienced, hence, Shakti is accepted as a personal Goddess — the primal energy.

The purpose of Shakti worship is to elevate human consciousness to a higher level, by following the lead of one who has tried the experiment and has succeeded.

In worship one proceeds from the outer square to the central point: this worship leads to the awakening of the *Kundalini* or Serpent Power lying coiled in the muladhara chakra. Serpent power is a universal principle: having created the human body it coils itself at the base and sleeps. It is roused deliberately by asanas, physical exercises in Hatha Yoga, but also by the power of Bhakti or Jnana yoga, the former by devotion and the latter by knowledge.

The sexo-yogic (coitus) way, purely Tantric, is another method. It is what is considered as Tantra , but it is only one of the methods in awakening the Kundalini, the Serpent Power.

The awakening of the *Kundalini* is the beginning of spiritual consciousness. This union with Shiva in the sahasrara chakra is the consumation of Shakti worship.

Kama-Kala

8

Kama-Kala

Kama-kala, the fundamental principle of all existence and experience, is an integral and basic part of the Sri Chakra worship. It is the fundamental theme or philosophy of the Sri Chakra mandala. It is a science and its representational art, the diagram, is its ritual technology, and its significance is the entire concept of the mystery.

This definition is complete for besides these two concepts of existence and experience, which emerge as one in their union — inseparable aspects of life — there is nothing else. Existence equals experience; experience equals existence. Its ramifications cover the entire phenomenal universe and of being.

The Mother Goddess is the basis of this principle. She embodies the whole principle, and for this reason she is called Tripura-Sundari or Lalita — the Ravisher.

'Kama' means desire; 'ka' means emanation; and 'la' means return or withdrawal to its source. This is the pulse-beat of the mystery of life, and this pulse-beat is cyclical like the throbbing of the human heart.

Some authors give other interpretations to Kama-kala: they regard Kama as Shiva and Kala as Shakti; and Shiva as 'Being' is equated with 'existence' and Shakti as 'Bliss' with 'experience'. And therefore the Shiva-Shakti yoga is Kama-kala.

In Tantric literature and Vedic text the word 'kama' means 'urge' or 'impulsion'. It is regarded as the 'seed' of the mind and also the instrument of differentiation. It is described as causing the original 'stress' or movement, but it is also described as a throb (*spanda*) which brought about sound (*nada*) which in turn brought about the phenomenal universe.

Apparently there was only a solitary dot* which inherently has three *gunas* or modes: sattvic (stable), rajasic (dynamic) and tamasic (inert). The matrix is the Mother Goddess, but in the three modes she represents sattvic, the rajasic by Shakti, and the tamasic by Shiva. The last two are her emanations or manifestations.

Note* There is another interpretation, probably an old one. In a state of repose and balance the yoni represents the circle, and the dot in the middle the *linga*; the *yoni* is the womb of *prakriti*, the female principle, which gives rise to all vibration and movement. In a state of activity the circle or *yoni* is transformed into the primary triangle, the source of manifestation which incorporates everything. In the new version it is the dot that is transformed into a triangle.

Evolutionary Process
The KAMA Stage

In the beginning was the Void, often described as watery, and hence, it is not really a void; it is not a void because there is a solitary tiny dot, but it appears that it was created and sprang up in the void. It is called bindu in Sanskrit. The bindu has the potential of giving birth to the phenomenal universe. It contains Reality, Cit-Sat-Ananda — Being-Consciousness-Bliss. This is embodied in the Mother Goddess.

In the withdrawal of the cosmos the bindu retained the shape of Mt. Meru, triangular with three essences of Being-Consciousness-Bliss, which are transmuted into three modes or basic elements of the cosmos: sattva, rajasa, and tamasa, or again as light, energy and sound. In this Reality the bindu is existence and experience. In its being it exists and with its consciousness it experiences. It is always in bliss. In Reality therefore the essence of everything is preexistent: they exist as essences or concepts before creation. They exist in a potential state in the bindu formed by Being-Consciousness-Bliss, which as modes of existence, i.e., as sattva, rajasa and tamasa are in perfect equilibrium, and in this condition there is no motion, no vibration, only a deep profound stillness, yet amidst this placid state is Being-Consciousness-Bliss.

This threefold aspect of the bindu, which also represents the evolutionary process, the process of preservation and the withdrawal process, is called Kama-kala. This is the fundamental theme of Tantrism. Its whole philosophy, science and worship is based on this. It is the principle for self-realization, enlightenment and salvation.

Man appears to have been ejected out of paradise and now must search for the return path, and this he has found in Tantra. But man, on the return trip, must journey alone. It is like man has lost his beloved, and is in the process of searching for the route back to her.

Man was ejected out of paradise when in its appointed time — everything is in its appointed time — Desire or Passion sprang up in the sattvic mode of the Mother Goddess. This is kama, the First Principle, to emerge in the form of a 'seed', the origin of Mind — the instrument of differentiation. It throbbed of its own accord, without any extraneous cause, stimulus or agency: this surge of consciousness was prompted solely by its nature.

The condition before the upsurge of Desire was tamasic — asleep or inert — a condition that is also sattvic or stable, but not rajasic or dynamic. The three modes or gunas are described as in perfect balance in this condition, but tamasic is dominant sustained and reinforced by sattva, which provides stability. It is at rest, a state equated with Shiva, the male principle; but nothing is definite with the Mother Goddess in the whole realm, for everything is happening all at once, spontaneously and instantaneously. And so paradoxically it is at rest yet also in motion; and this is mainly because of the presence of the dynamic female principle called Shakti

Although the dot, the *parabindu* or *mahabindu* in Sanskrit means a 'drop' and 'nada' is sound, in Tantra they are regarded as technical terms denoting evolutionary processes. Involved in the *bindu* is the process of a point unfolding into the universe, and nada is regarded as the thrill of the primary impulse towards evolution or manifestation. Yet, this thrill is also regarded as sound — the *sphota*, the inaudible sound.

With the Absolute, however, there is nothing conclusive: either element turns into modes or acquire different roles or functions or meaning. Sanskrit terms are like this: they take on manifold meanings or significance, and often it is and at the same time it is not. This is perhaps because of the principle of transformation; thus the illusion, the handiwork of Maya. They are all in the process of evolving and becoming. There is no definite conclusion:

it is all open-ended for other possibilities.

In modern science a dot turns into a wave. In Tantrism a dot turns into three dots, and like a magic they turn into lines forming a triangle, transmuting into other modes or functions until the whole phenomenal universe is created. This is the reason why the yantra, which is linear is important: it makes up the geometric patterns in the mandala, the very form of the Mother Goddess.

The throb (spanda) disturbed the placid condition, and the three gunas lost their balance and fell apart whirling in the process. In their whirling motion is their functions: *sattva* is the ascending or centripetal tendency, a cohesive force directed towards unity and stability; *rajasa* is the revolving tendency which gives impetus to the creative forces; *tamasa* is the descending or centrifugal force, with an outward motion, the force which causes dissolution.

When they fall they are so arranged that they convey the idea of a triangle: one above and two below. This is the form of the Mother Goddess. This is the kama-kala, which never alters its shape or form.

Desire or passion throbs — the initial primal sound — in the sattvic mode, and in the process light is ignited, which indicates that the Void is in absolute darkness. The light is attracted (vimarsa) to Shakti, the rajasic dynamic mode, which is aroused and provides energy to it. In its movement towards Shakti its image (light) is reflected back to it and it becomes self-conscious. It acquires the quality of polarity, the potential of being an instrument of differentiation and of establishing a relationship.

With energy the light (prakasa) now turns into a 'sperm'. Now sattva with rajasa becomes Shakti, the female principle, which, awakened from its sleep emits a sibilant hissing sound (the consonants) as it moves towards the tamasic mode, Shiva, the male principle, containing the vowels.

When it plunges into the tamasic bindu it swells, which indicates it is not an explosion but an implosion. The implosion produced the primary vowel sound of 'A' (in the ajna chakra in the forehead); the second sound produced is 'Ha' (in the visuddha chakra in the region of the throat); and the third sound is 'Ham' (in the anahata chakra in the region of the heart). This is the sound produced by a combination of consonants and vowels, which in turn projected the phenomenal universe in the form of waves of light and sound.

In Sanskrit the sound is the sacred Primal Sound OM, that sustains and preserves the universe. This is the reason why the alphabet is said to cover the whole range of the phenomenal cosmos. Hence, the significance of the mantra. OM is the framework of the phenomenal experience. The entire experiential world is based on this mantra. This is actually the kama-kala, the basic theme in Sri Chakra. Sound is likened to the mirror reflecting the form of everything, and this is the background for all phenomenal emanation.

This is the Primary Chakra, the thousand-petalled lotus, the gate or opening through which the cosmos was born. This is the residence of the Mother Goddess located at the top of the universe; it is called Mt. Meru. It is through this opening that the light, sound and energy (desire) burst out, eventually being transformed into the phenomenal universe.

Everything, therefore is made of 'waves', vibrations of light and sound, and the whole universe is sustained and preserved by the Primal Audible Sound OM or AUM, which represents the three divinities or Hindu trinity of Brahma, Vishnu and Shiva. It represents also the kama-kala.

In the kama-kala the Sri Chakra is linked up with the moon and the sun, but more with the moon, which is represented as fifteen digits in the form of letters involving vowels and consonants which are accommodated in the lotus petals in the yantra.

Preservation
The KA Stage

At the beginning the Mother Goddess sits on her throne with four legs representing the male gods: Brahama, Vishnu, Shiva and Sadashiva, each of which symbolizes emanation, preservation, withdrawal and retention. They represent the main four principles of kama-kala. The fifth principle belongs to the Mother Goddess and this is the potential re-manifestation of the phenomenal universe.

The male divinities are passive, inert; it is only when the Mother Goddess inspires them that they become active, and begin to create the phenomenal universe and everything in it including Man. The essence of man and of woman, however, in existentialism, has always been there, and has experienced being in paradise with the Mother Goddess.

Human beings, the male and the female, are all a blending of the union of Shiva and Shakti. Thus man is inert, passive, and woman is dynamic and creative, inspiring. It is her inspiration that makes the male active and he begins to participate in life. Both feel lonely and they come together for life, but they have an innate feeling of having known paradise from which they had been ejected. So in life there comes a time when they start to seek that which they have lost.

In Tantrism the 'return path' has been found: it is in worship. In worship they follow the return path, the process of involution: the reabsorption in the Source. It is to disappear into it in a blissful state of being.

The way has taken a long time in being discovered and evolving and crystallizing into a certainty realized in the Tantric doctrine of the 'Divine Within' in which the *participation mystique* takes place. The pilgrim must take the route back alone. The possibility of union with the Mother Goddess, of seeing her, urges him on and need not wait for the withdrawal of the cosmos to be with her.

Withdrawal
The LA Stage

When the sound vibration disappears the phenomenal universe is dissolved, the three *gunas*, again in perfect balance, are withdrawn.

Tantrism emphasizes in its yantra and mantra the integrated structure of the universe. And it holds that the integrity of the structure is fundamentally based on its functional unity — the unity of direction — which is mainly due to the presence and power of the Mother Goddess.

Lincoln Barnett in *The Universe and Dr. Einstein* wrote that the universe is progressing toward an ultimate 'heat death' or as it is technically defined, to a condition of 'maximum entropy'. "Time itself will come to an end. For entropy points the direction of time... Entropy is the measure of randomness... When there no longer is any sequence of cause and effect – in short when the universe has run down, there will be no direction to time, there will be no time. And there is no way of avoiding this destiny."

This is similar to the view held by Tantrism in regard to the end of the universe. When the unity of direction of the universe is lost it will then fold up and withdraw into the original bindu. The play of the Mother Goddess is over. Until in its appointed time it will spring up again through love – Desire.

The return trip therefore is called the Yoga of Love.

Only through Desire can one retrace the steps back to the Beloved.

Worship

The Mother Goddess is called *Tripura* because she has also three forms in which she is worshipped: 1) physical in the human form either at home or in temples; 2) subtle or verbal form with mantra by inner sacrifice (*antar-yoga*) with meditation upon its symbolism; 3) Mental or transcendental (*mansa, para*) in the abstract form but with all-inclusive power, with the body of the worshipper as the temple of the Mother Goddess.

Worship of the yantra for material or spiritual favor is external worship; mantra worship is in the form of meditation: this is internal worship; in the third form the worshipper must contemplate the entire triangle — the kama-kala — as his own body: the top as his head and the two dots below as the two sides of his body; the straight line at the base as his foundational posture, the line to the left going up to the apex as his effort in *sadhana* (meditation); the line to the right coming down from the apex as the descent of grace (*anugraha*) of the Mother Goddess.

In kama-kala meditation the initiate is thus admonished:
> 'From my true Being the universe has emerged,
> subsisist on IT, and dissolve into IT.'

This experience is called Sarvatma-bhava:
> 'Myself is the self of All'.

ANALYSIS

Analysis

Everything, the phenomenal universe of existence and experience, is the result of the Shiva-Shakti Yoga, the union of the male and female principles, caused by the sudden upsurge of desire, which precipitates the evolutionary process of creation.

Existence and experience are fundamentally based on the Shiva-Shakti Yoga, and when this knot is untangled the whole structure of the universe is withdrawn back into its pristine primal state: a condition of profound stillness yet blissful existence.

This is the concept of paradise of man. Along with the cosmos he was born out of the blissful union of Shiva and Shakti. His essence is bliss, but he has forgotten to be blissful. His experience in human existence is miserable. He feels wretched, but intuition tells him not to despair, for there is salvation.

In his worship he stumbles upon Tantra, which shows him the way to liberation. The Sri Chakra offers him a passage to the eternal, but he must undergo rigorous training before he could take it up. On the doctrine of the 'Divine Within' he begins to trace his way back to the Source — the blissful state in paradise. It is to experience self-realization. And in the *participation mystique* he will confirm the presence of the divine essence in his being.

In worship the process of evolution is reversed and he follows the process of involution. He alone must attempt it, and he turns into a pilgrim. He goes on a pilgrimage as a lover seeking for his beloved. To make the journey back to the Source he has to purify his body and mind. Purity is essential; it is indispensable to a successful journey into the spiritual world. It is to be able to identify with the Goddess' retinue divinities, the *yogins* guarding the way and be accepted by them. But he must have love or passion, a desire to see or be in union with her.

And for her, the beloved, he must be fearless, willing to leave everything, the world, renounce his earthly existence, even his life for her. So he has to be pure physically and spiritually. His intentions have to be pure and honorable.

Revulsion he experiences in his earthly life makes him fall in love with the Mother Goddess. Desire springs up to join her. Love, desire, is a powerful creative force. It is the basis of life. In his worship, with desire in his heart, he awakens the *Kundalini*, the Serpent Power, who is Shakti. His consciousness must identify with Shakti, the female principle, and must accompany her in her upward rise and movement towards Shiva, the male principle, in the *saharara chakra*.

He becomes one with Shakti in its movement upwards towards the center. And when Shakti reaches the sahasrara chakra it is not Shiva that is seated there, but the Mother Goddess. As a divine manifestation Shakti dissolves in union with him, and the pilgrim experiences union with the Mother Goddess. In the embrace of the Beloved, in yoga, everything for a moment is not only forgotten but dissolved: his mind and body, his whole existence, the whole phenomenal universe, and only there is an observing and feeling spirit left. Thus the experienced bliss in yoga is remembered.

With this experience confirming the doctrine of the Divine Within the pilgrim becomes godly. He is self-realized and enlightened.

In the involution process it is actually like untangling the Shiva-Shakti Yoga for the withdrawal of the entire phenomenal cosmos of existence and experience until there is nothing left except for pure consciousness in a blissful state. In this state the Mother Goddess and Shiva are together, but not in union. The Goddess is seated on Shiva until desire, an emotional surge, precipitates creation. She becomes Shakti and joins Shiva: in their union there is a burst of bliss and the whole phenomenal universe of existence and experience is born.

This is what happens on the return journey to the Source, when self-realization is attained. The universe, everything, ceases to exist. It is mind-blowing. In self-realization there is a temporary disappearance of everything. There remains only pure consciousness that witnesses the experience.

In the union it appears that Shiva is forgotten. In Tantrism this is *maithuna* (coitus), a divine connubium. In this blissful self-realization the lover has found his beloved, the Mother Goddess. With the female initiate self-realization is attained in union with Shiva. It is Shiva she will encounter in the sahasrara chakra.

BIBLIOGRAPHY

Chetananda, Swami, *Avadhuta Gita* (Dattareya), Advaita Ashrama, Calcutta, India, 1988.

Das Gupta, S.N., *Hindu Mysticism*, Motilal Banarsi Das Publications, Delhi, 1992.

Gosh, Sri Aurobindo, *Bengali Writings*, Sri Aurobindo Trust, Pondicherry, India, 1991.

Jansen, Eva Rudy, *The Book of Hindu Imagery*, Binkey Kok Publications, Diever, Holland, 1993.

Maury, Curt, *Folk Origin of Indian Art*, Columbia University Press, USA., 1969.

Mookerjee, Ajit & Khanna, Madhu, *The Tantric Way*, Thames and Hudson, London, 1993 reprint.

Prabhavananda, Swami, *Patanjali Yoga*, Ramakrishna Math, Madra, India, 1991.

Rao, Ramachandra, *Sri Chakra*, Sri Satguru Publications, Delhi, India, 1989

Santiago, J.R., *Sacred Symbols of Hinduism*, Book Faith India, Delhi, 1998

Saraswati, Swami satya Prakash, *Agnihotra*, Allahabad, India, 1985.

Tapasyananda, Swami, *Sri Lalita Sahasranama*, Sri Ramakrishna Math, Madras, India, 1993.

Tapasyananda, Swami, *Saundarya Lahiri* (Inundation of Divine Splendor), Sri Ramakrishna Math, Madras, India, 1987.

Tucci, Guiseppe, *Sacred Symbols: Mandala*, Thames and Hudson, London.
" " , *The Theory and Practice of the Mandala*, trans. A.H. Borderick, Rider & Company, London, 1974.

Vimalananda, Swami, *Sri Lalithambika*, Sri Ramakrishna Math, Madras, 1984.
Yogananda, Paramahansa, *Autobiography of a Yogi*, Jaico Publishing House, Bombay, 1997.

Other Titles in This Series by Book Faith India

1. SACRED SYMBOLS OF BUDDHISM — J.R. Santiago
2. SACRED SYMBOLS OF HINDUISM — J.R. Santiago
3. KRIYA YOGA : THE SCIENCE OF SELF-REALIZATION — J.R. Santiago
4. SACRED MANDALA OF BUDDHISM — J.R. Santiago
5. THANGKA: THE SACRED PAINTING OF TIBET — J.R. Santiago

For Catalog and more information Mail or Fax to:

PILGRIMS BOOK HOUSE
Mail Order, P.O.Box 3872, Kathmandu, Nepal
Fax: 977-1-424943
e-mail: mail@pilgrims.wlink.com.np
website : www.pilgrimsbooks.com